The Local Union

REVISED EDITION

The Local Union

REVISED EDITION

Leonard R. Sayles

Columbia University

George Strauss

University of California, Berkeley

Harcourt, Brace & World, Inc.

New York / Chicago / San Francisco / Atlanta

Cover photo courtesy of *N.M.U. Pilot*.

Library of Congress Catalog Card Number: 67–17182

Printed in the United States of America

To our Wives Helene and Risha

Preface

The local union is the key point of contact between the union member and his union. In fact, to many members the local *is* the union. Certainly it is on the local level that the union member participates in union activities, and it is the local officers who service his needs. Our study is concerned with the local union as an ongoing institution, with the attitudes and activities of the people who comprise it (both the active leaders and the inactive members), with the pressures to which they are subject, and with their relations with the outside world, particularly the company. We sought to look at the local as a whole, not just at a segment of it.

For these reasons we believe our study is of interest even beyond the area of industrial relations, seeking as it does to describe a complex organization in all its ramifications. Furthermore, our "behavioral" approach, with its emphasis on the interaction of people, is illustrative of a method of analysis which can be applied to many sorts of organization.

When we undertook this study, research for which lasted five years, there was a tendency to undervalue the role of the local union relative to that of the more visible and powerful national union. In succeeding years the unique contribution of the local and of its grievance process to the vigor of American industrial relations has come to be more widely appreciated. Overseas, the frequent absence of this type of membership unit leads to a very different pattern of membership participation.

Our research was based on participant observation and informal interviewing in twenty local unions.[1] We tried to live with our situations, observing membership, executive board, and steward council meetings as well as countless informal caucuses and bull sessions. Many of our contacts were made over beer at local bars or at members' homes. Our goal was to obtain insight in depth and to develop real rapport with the people whose problems we were trying to understand. As a consequence, our findings are somewhat more impressionistic than those of later studies which have made use of survey questionnaires and statistical sampling techniques. (Sayles did make use of special projective tests designed to elicit members' reactions toward their union and its grievance procedures.[2])

Though our original work involved us with the building-trades and white-collar unions, the findings here presented relate primarily to unions in manufacturing industries. The patterns of life in building-trades unions, in the Teamsters, and in service-trades unions generally differ greatly.[3] Although we studied unions in the garment industry, our findings in this area are only partially applicable to large amalgamated unions which cover a number of plants or work places.[4] Normally, of the unions mentioned, the first two—building-trades and the Teamsters—have strong business agents. In many cases, members must go through union-controlled hiring halls to get their jobs; moreover, the wide dispersion of work places makes communications within the union more difficult. All these factors affect the character of internal union life generally.

On the other hand, although the work of white-collar and professional employees differs greatly from that of blue-collar workers, our findings seem to apply quite closely to the former groups as well.

The narrow focus of this book should be kept in mind, since there is a danger that by concentrating on details we lose our feeling for the whole.

---

[1] For further discussion of our research methodology, see the appendix to the first edition of this work as well as George Strauss, "Direct Observation as a Source of Quasi-Sociometric Information," *Sociometry,* Vol. 15, No. 1 (February 1962), pp. 141–45; and John Gullahorn and George Strauss, "The Field Worker in Union Research," in *Human Organization Research,* Richard Adams and Jack Preiss, Eds. (Homewood, Ill.: Dorsey, 1960).

[2] See Leonard R. Sayles, "Field Use of Projective Methods: A Case Example," *Sociology and Social Research,* Vol. 38, No. 3 (January 1954), pp. 168–73.

[3] For some of our work in these areas, see George Strauss, *Unions in the Building Trades* (Buffalo: University of Buffalo Press, 1958); "White Collar Unions are Different!" *Harvard Business Review,* Vol. 32 (September 1954), pp. 73–82; "Professionalism and Occupational Associations," *Industrial Relations,* Vol. 2, No. 3 (May 1963), pp. 7–31; "Professional or Employee Oriented: Dilemma for Engineering Unions," *Industrial and Labor Relations Review,* Vol. 17, No. 4 (July 1964), pp. 519–33; "The AAUP as a Professional Occupational Association," *Industrial Relations,* Vol. 5, No. 1 (October 1965), pp. 128–40; and David Kockery and George Strauss, "The Non-Profit Hospital and the Union," *Buffalo Law Review,* Vol. 7 (Winter 1960), pp. 255–82.

[4] For an excellent analysis of the internal dynamics of large, multiplant unions, see Alice Cook, *Union Democracy: Practice and Ideal* (Ithaca, N.Y.: Cornell University Press, 1963).

Indeed, as one local leader wrote, after reading the first draft of this volume: ". . . If it were not for the fact that union leaders know and feel that they are improving the conditions of their fellow men, the internal strife and obstacles explained so well in your book might well bring on the destruction of the labor movement."

This is the second and somewhat abridged edition of a book first published by Harper & Brothers. Although fourteen years have passed since publication of the original work, it is still so pertinent to its subject that it has been necessary to rewrite substantially only one chapter—Chapter 11. Instead of interlarding references to recent research throughout the book we have added an epilogue, which lists major recent changes that have affected the local union and the more important research reported since 1953.

Part of this work was done for doctoral theses at the Massachusetts Institute of Technology, and the remainder was done under a grant from the W. T. Grant Foundation at the New York State School of Industrial and Labor Relations, Cornell University.

Charles A. Myers of the Massachusetts Institute of Technology and William F. Whyte of Cornell helped us greatly in the design and analysis of our research. We were indeed fortunate to have such guidance at the beginning of our professional careers, and our gratitude for their insight and patience grows over the years. Both should have shared in the research award, presented to us in 1952 by the Society for the Psychological Study of Social Issues, which designated this work the best contribution to "the scientific understanding of labor-management relations."

"Who are we not to help those who are in trouble?" According to a recent article in the *New York Times,* Joe Granto gave this characteristic response when asked to organize assistance for the family of a migrant Puerto Rican farm worker killed in a fire. Joe (and his wife, Catherine) were extremely helpful to us when we were doing our original study, and we were moved to learn that after fifteen years Joe has not changed. May we express our gratitude for his assistance and the assistance of many like him, and our respect for their values.

Finally, may we repeat the dedication to the first edition:

To Mike, Big, Eddie, Henry, Frank, Art, Leo, Al, Bill, Jimmy, Sally, Gordon, Grace, Buddy, Blanche, Larry, Joe (and, of course, Catherine), and countless other union friends whose help made this work possible.

We hope that in the long run work like this will develop a social science which will help build the better world to which you are dedicated.

Leonard R. Sayles   *New York*

George Strauss   *Berkeley*

Contents

Contents

The Local Union

REVISED EDITION

1

An Overview of the Local

This book seeks to describe local industrial unions—their members, officers, and stewards, and how these are affected by the factories in which they work. It is concerned with the human-relations problems of the officers and the rank and file faced with the complicated task of negotiating with management and keeping their union going.

When the proverbial man in the street thinks of the word "union" he thinks of the International and the men like Hoffa and Reuther, who make the headlines. But for the average member in the factory, his union is his *local*—and when he talks about the union he talks about his *local* officers and his *local's* problems.

The union member may point with pride to Walter Reuther, but he knows Bill Smith, his steward, and can talk to him personally. While his basic wage may be determined in a paneled conference room a thousand miles away, the steward who handles his everyday problems with the foreman symbolizes the tangible services provided by the union. The local which argues for him on the question of a 35-cent shortage in his paycheck, an extra twenty pieces on his work load, or his right to ten years, six months, and four days of seniority is the organization which matters most.

The union does not exist in a vacuum. It reflects the needs of the workers it serves, the rewards and punishments they receive in their industrial life.

1

Yet, despite this, the union is not a "way of life." Only for a small group of its members does it provide important social satisfactions. But the union's objective is not purely that of maximizing wages and job opportunities. For once, the law comes close to reality. The union is fundamentally a "collective bargaining representative," with a twofold purpose: (1) to provide workers with an opportunity to participate in determining the conditions under which they work, because they want the results of such participation in terms of better working conditions and because they want participation for its own sake, and (2) to afford workers an effective channel whereby they can protest conditions which they think are unfair.

The Structure of the Local

As background for later discussions of this internal life, the following section presents a simple, unfortunately incomplete, structural description of the types of locals we studied. These descriptions apply only to industrial locals and primarily to those functioning in the manufacturing industries.

No two locals are alike. A tremendous range of factors affects their organization and functioning: the International to which they belong, the industry whose workers they represent, the section of the country in which they are located, their size, and many others.

Size   During World War II, several locals pressed the 100,000-member mark. Many have a membership of less than 25. This very range in size illustrates the difficulties of generalizing about union locals. The description which follows relates primarily to locals of a size from 500 members to 2000, the type with which our research has been primarily concerned.

Jurisdiction   Local unions have widely differing jurisdictions. Some encompass just a single plant. However, with a trend toward white-collar organization, there are often two or more locals in the same plant—one for production workers and the other for clericals. Frequently there are separate locals for members of skilled crafts within these same plants. Further, in the building and service trades, where the employer unit is small, craft locals representing an entire community are the rule. However, only a small proportion of our research was in this area.

General structure   The local is the basic building block of the union. Of course, higher in the union structure are the various city councils, joint boards, and district and state organizations, and the Internationals, as well as the great confederation, the A.F.L.-C.I.O. But the average member can participate in these only indirectly through his officers and delegates.

Below these levels, most locals provide for departmental meetings which may be called by the local president, the chief steward, or a portion of the membership. Such meetings are in fact held infrequently and are seldom more than informal "gripe" sessions. The real political life in most locals revolves around the meetings of the officers or of the local as a whole. Where the local includes more than one plant there are usually shop committee and shop meetings for each plant.

Constitutions   Presumably, the formal organization of the local is determined by its constitution. However, to concentrate on this is to concentrate on the static shell of a highly dynamic institution. Many unions are more democratic than their constitutions might indicate; others are less so. For instance, the International Ladies' Garment Workers' Union had an Objections Committee with power to eliminate "unqualified" candidates. This powerful weapon was little used, perhaps because the Communists, against whom it was directed, are now so weak.

Union meetings   The membership is regarded in most constitutions as the sovereign governing body of the local. There are few locals which do not at least go through the motions of holding meetings. As far as we have observed, most union meetings function vigorously and democratically.

Of course, the act of holding meetings does not automatically make a local democratic. As we shall see, only a small portion of the membership attends. Still, as long as meetings are held, they provide a forum within which the dissatisfied member can agitate for change.

The officers   A few locals boast officers with designations as chief engineer, sentinel, and conductor, titles recalling the fact that many of our older unions were once secret, benevolent, and fraternal organizations. (Indeed, a few still retain their elaborate ceremonies and secret rituals.) But most locals give their officers more prosaic names: president, vice-president, recording secretary, financial secretary, and treasurer. A few miscellaneous officers such as guides, sergeants-at-arms, and trustees (who audit the books) are added for good measure. Almost all of these continue to work in the plant; their union activity is conducted in their leisure time, or in a few "lost-time hours" during regular working hours.

The larger locals may have one or more full-time employees or "pork choppers." Usually these are called business agents. Some locals put their president or secretary-treasurer on the payroll as well. Where the local has a business agent and an unpaid president, the business agent usually has the greater prestige and authority. He is the one who negotiates contracts and handles important grievances.

Elections   With a few exceptions, union elections are conducted in the democratic tradition. The length of the union officer's term of office has been increasing. In the early days of unionism many officers held their positions for only six months. Until recently a one-year period was common. Now, many unions seek greater stability by holding elections every two years.[1]

Executive committee   The executive committee consists of the principal officers of the local. There is often some attempt to distribute these offices among the various departmental groups so that the majority of their interests will be represented.

The executive board determines general union policy. It has sole control over "administrative business" such as financial questions, community relations, the writing of by-laws, appointments of committees and delegates. In theory its action is subject to final approval by the membership but, as will be seen, this is often a formality.

Grievance committee   One of the union's most important functions is the processing of grievances or worker and union complaints against management. In some locals, grievances are handled by the executive committee; in others, by a separate "grievance" or "negotiating" committee. Where these functions are separated, the divided authority often leads to jealousy. However, this is often mitigated by overlapping membership. The president, among other officials, is almost always a member of both committees.

Chief stewards and stewards   The executive committee or the negotiating committee operates at the highest step in the grievance procedure at the local level. Below it are the "noncoms" of the union, the chief stewards (sometimes called committeemen or grievancemen), and below them the stewards.[2] Chief stewards' constituencies range from 30 to 300. The number of workers represented by a single steward varies from approximately ten to fifty members. Chief stewards typically bargain with their management counterparts, the superintendents—and stewards with foremen.

Miscellaneous committees   The picture would not be complete without mentioning such bodies as the activities committee, which plans picnics, dances, athletic events, and lotteries; the welfare committee, which visits the sick, sends flowers to the deceased, and makes small grants to the needy; the organizing committee (where there is no union shop); the education and political committee; and sometimes, a special job evaluation or incentive rate committee. Normally the members of these committees are appointed by the president, subject to membership ratification. A majority of these committees

[1] The Landrum-Griffin Act specifies that, at a minimum, local unions must hold elections every three years, and national unions every five years.
[2] In the clothing trades, a shop chairman serves as grievance representative for a shop, which may be a large department or an entire small plant. Above him is the full-time business agent.

are relatively inactive. The positions are hard to fill, and anyone seriously interested can serve.

Recreation   A few unions try to provide a full recreational program for their members as well as protection at work. However, the locals we observed found it impractical to compete with the established social activities of the community. To be sure, a picnic for the entire family in the summer and a dance in the winter will be successful, particularly if the local itself foots a large share of the bill. In fact, it was not unusual to observe a union appropriating 10 per cent of its treasury for a social affair "so the members will feel they're getting something for their dues." Parties for the children at Christmas also are popular, but this was the extent of such social activities.

The field representative   The field representative (sometimes called staff or International representative) is appointed and paid by the International union. His function is to organize new locals and assist established ones to handle their affairs and deal with management. Where locals are small, one representative may serve a dozen locals. But if the local is large enough, a team of such staff men, as they are called, may be assigned to assist it.

The relative importance of the field representative differs widely in different Internationals. In craft unions the local's own business agent customarily handles most of the work. In the automobile and steel industries there are few paid business agents, and here the field representative plays a more important role. Even in these industries, they restrict themselves pretty largely to "collective bargaining" business (grievances and contract negotiations). Few locals will tolerate any interference with their internal administrative affairs.

The point at which the International enters contract negotiations (which is one way of measuring the autonomy of the local) necessarily varies in different situations, primarily for economic reasons. Building trades locals are given wide autonomy to determine their own economic policy. Pottery industry agreements, on the other hand, are negotiated on a nationwide basis. Many segments of American industry practice *pattern bargaining*. Here the contract terms negotiated with the larger companies are followed more or less faithfully by all the smaller firms, with the International taking the role of a policeman to make sure that the agreements do not deviate too far from the general "pattern." The obvious fear is that less militant locals would give their employers a lower wage bill than those who adhere closely to the pattern.

All in all, a substantial proportion of union members work under contracts negotiated by paid representatives of the national office. Contract writing and negotiation is a specialized art; local leaders are often glad to accept the assistance of experts. As a result, in most locals the International has an important say in determining the type of contract negotiated.

However, except in matters involving competitive differences in wages or piece rates, the International is usually anxious to encourage independence and initiative on the part of the local. International field representatives have limited budgets. If each local called upon them whenever it had a problem or grievance, their servicing job would be impossible. Therefore, they prefer to concentrate on organizing and on the more important grievance appeal cases which might set a precedent affecting a number of locals.

Conclusion

This study deals with two distinctive yet related aspects of the local union: (1) the interrelations of workers and work groups and their union with management and the work environment, and (2) the internal organizational aspects of the union's structure.

In the ensuing chapters it will often be difficult to separate these two categories of union activity: *collective bargaining business* and *internal administrative business*.

Collective bargaining business relates to such things as hours and conditions of work, rates of pay, seniority, promotions, etc.—things which concern the worker's individual relationship to the company. The internal administrative business relates to the management of the union—matters such as elections to union office, appointment of committees, and expenditure of money. Throughout, we shall stress that the functioning of the union represents a fine balance among needs of individuals, those attracted and those repelled by union office, the economic and political interests of specific work groups seeking to influence the local, and the needs of the institution itself as expressed in the recurring organizational problems. All of these, somehow intertwined with the goals of management and the firm, produce a dynamic, fascinating panorama of human organization.

2

The Grievance Procedure in Action

Union-management relations are far from static. The common stereotype of an increasingly aggressive union confronting an ever-defensive management is an exaggeration. Of course, the first bargaining sessions between the company and a newly certified union are often bitter. However, in most cases, as both sides gain experience with collective bargaining, some kind of accommodation supplants the initial antagonisms.

Recent years have seen increasing interest in the process by which open industrial warfare is transformed into "working harmony" and "industrial peace." Naturally, as there are changes in the external relation between union and management, there are corresponding adjustments within the political life of the local. These will be considered in succeeding chapters. This chapter is devoted primarily to a description of some of the salient features of the changing union-management relationship as they affect the local's officers.

The Organizing Period

Men join unions to improve their standard of living. But even more they are seeking individual dignity and control of their environment. They are protesting what they feel is unjust treatment and looking to the union to protect them against inequities, fears, and insecurity. In the majority of cases, latent discontent existed long before the union organizer came along; his job was merely to channel these feelings toward the union.

In the organizing campaign, union solidarity is built up at the expense of loyalty to management. The new union is vehemently antimanagement, as it must be to gain a solid foothold in what is usually an antiunion environment. In this first period the workers rid themselves of long frustration through their aggressiveness against the "boss." Often there is a bitter strike before the first contract is signed.

The organizers seek to dramatize to the rank and file their willingness to press any and all claims. Practically every decision the company makes is challenged—even those with which the union leaders themselves are satisfied.

During this period grievances are, in fact, "tests of strength whose real intent is to strengthen one party and weaken another . . . the real issue is the struggle for power."[1] The union engages in an all-out effort to increase its power relative to that of management and to increase the number of its adherents in the shop.

The Beginnings of Industrial Peace

This type of unregulated warfare cannot persist indefinitely. As Harbison and Coleman suggest:

> As armed truce relationships mature, however, the system of grievance settlement tends to become very orderly and businesslike. The company gradually gets its supervisory forces trained in the principles and practices of dealing with union functionaries. The union finds that it gains little by taking up "screwy grievances" only to lose them in the costly process of arbitration. As key grievance cases are settled, precedents are established which set the pattern for the disposition of similar types of grievances. By the process of pushing here and probing there, the contract gets "pretty well explored." In this way, a body of plant common laws is developed. The union officers and company representatives become, in effect, "shop lawyers" who are experts in fine legal technicalities and precedents. Indeed, the grievance process ultimately becomes so highly institutionalized that neither side wants to upset the body of common law which has been hammered out in years of grievance handling.[2]

Thus, even where the parties are opposed to each other there is a tendency to establish regularized rules of competition. Within the union, for instance, limited time and money soon force the leaders to become selective about which grievances they might process. Only those which improve their strategic position are pushed.

[1] Frank C. Pierson, *Collective Bargaining Systems* (Washington, D.C.: American Council on Public Affairs, 1942), p. 12.
[2] John R. Coleman and Frederick H. Harbison, *Goals and Strategy in Collective Bargaining* (New York: Harper & Row, 1951), pp. 41–42.

In addition, the union is sometimes required to discipline its members in order to make a more effective fighting force. Unauthorized strikes are frowned upon as a dissipation of union strength. No union can afford the drain of continuous warfare. Relative peace between annual or biannual contract negotiations increases the likelihood that the rank and file will be ready for "war" if it comes—and that anticipations are not aroused which cannot be satisfied. Union officials who earlier may have spent much of their time agitating the members now find themselves forced to urge patience and restraint.

As Bakke points out, perhaps the primary need of the parties in a collective bargaining relationship is that of *survival*.[3] As long as the union is afraid that management is attempting to destroy its organization and as long as management fears that the union's demands will be so extreme as to force it out of business, they cannot settle down to harmonious working relations. Stability appears only when each side takes into account the institutional or survival needs of the other.

Thus, as the atmosphere clears, the stage is set for the development of more "mature relationships." Even though industrial peace is rarely reached in a single jump, the parties may take tentative steps in that direction.

Adjustment Between Individuals

With experience comes an awareness on both sides that not all subjects with which they deal involve areas of conflict. Many problems that reach the bargaining table are mutual problems, and both parties can benefit directly from an appropriate settlement. For example, management wants to decrease tardiness and absenteeism by introducing a more desirable work schedule. The union can contribute to a plan that will minimize employee discontent and wage losses and facilitate an easy adjustment to new working hours.

A negotiator can do a substantially better bargaining job if he knows how his opposite will react to various words and situations. When verbal warfare is substituted for picketing, personal relationships develop inevitably among a small group of key local negotiators who have the authority to make decisions. These men see each other almost daily and soon become familiar with one another's idiosyncrasies.

Management representatives quickly learn to differentiate between the grievances on which the union leaders face strong political pressures and those on which they are merely going through the motions of pressing. At the same time, the union officers recognize that there are certain areas in which management cannot afford to "lose face" even though it is wrong. A shrewd management learns not to embarrass union officials before a close election; in the

---

[3] E. Wight Bakke, *Mutual Survival: The Goal of Union and Management* (New Haven Labor and Management Center, Yale University, 1946).

same way, astute union leaders realize that personnel directors must have some kind of results to show the company president.[4]

We have observed many episodes like the one reflected in the following statement by a union leader to a personnel director:

> Look, Bill, we'll admit that Charlie Jones was drunk last week. Frankly we don't have a leg to stand on. If you'll take it easy on him—after all this is his first case—we'll waive the formal hearing. And that'll save you a lot of time and money.

Some bargains are implicit. The union may not press its advantage to the fullest in one case in the hope of a similar consideration on the part of management later on. As one union leader said in discussing a seniority case:

> We won our principle. That's what's important. I'm not going to pull Smith off the job just because the company made a mistake. If I make a concession now, they'll do me a favor later on.

Another leader commented:

> It's the spirit of the contract which counts, not the letter. If you're going to push for the last drop of blood, you can't expect consideration from management. Of course, I'm attacked for this by some of the hot heads, but I believe that live and let live pays off in the long run.

These are not collusive dealings but rather part of the flexible process by which both sides adjust to new problem situations which could not have been foreseen when the contract was written.

Even where the policy of top union and top management is still one of unwavering antagonism, lieutenants on the lower levels may find that accommodation is a policy which strengthens everyone's position. In a large plant which had experienced a number of wildcat strikes, for example, one of the most aggressive leaders admitted:

> Well, the super could have turned me in. But he didn't. He could have told the company that all morning I was going around organizing the fellows to walk off the job. But fortunately he's not that kind.
>
> For one thing, we get along pretty well. When I was first elected, I told him that the union could make things pretty tough unless he wanted to play along. Now I do something for him and he does something for me. We both bluff each other and it works pretty well.

Day-to-Day Collective Bargaining

The wide area of maneuver allowed by corporation and industry-wide contracts provides an invitation to management and union officials to make flexi-

---

[4] Another motivating factor may be the desire of local union leaders and plant managers to maintain their autonomy and to prevent interference from higher levels of authority in both organizations.

ble working arrangements. Perhaps from a legalistic point of view collective bargaining occurs only when the master contract is being negotiated. However, contracts having such broad coverage must of necessity be worded in general terms. A legal document drafted in a series of tense bargaining conferences cannot hope to spell out answers to all the countless problems which may arise before the new contract is written. At best it can only specify the major conditions of employment. The significance of any particular contract clause for an individual member or group is determined by its day-to-day application in the shop.

In matters such as seniority, job evaluation, and incentive rate setting, the contract often suggests merely the *method* of settlement or the standards to be used, rather than the settlement itself. Application of these clauses to specific conditions requires further negotiations and interpretations.

Work Rules

Since the momentous 116-day steel strike of 1959, students of industrial relations have come to recognize the importance of work rules in the day-to-day lives of employees. While not explicitly described in most contracts, a host of unwritten *ad hoc* agreements on how work is to be performed are developed by employees and their supervisors.

For example, airline "service representatives" (the girls who greet and assist airlines passengers) recently filed a grievance that management was requiring them to wear uniform hats that mussed their hair-do's;[5] More important work-rules issues concern how many men will compose a crew, the length of work breaks and wash-up time, and the dividing line between jobs (e.g., whether a stamping-machine operator should remove a jammed blank even though that is "maintenance work").

While these may not be part of the formal agreement, they quickly become part of the living contract that governs working relationships. Employees are quick to sense any change that makes their daily routine more painful, and they expect the local union to defend the rules they have grown used to. In turn, management often forgets the special circumstances under which they traded some privilege and accuse the employees of featherbedding by claiming the privilege as an "established" work rule.

> Example: in a large tire plant in the high sales years of 1955 and 1956, the foremen in the tire building department needed faster delivery of tread pieces to their tire builders. Instead of requiring the fork-lift drivers to make the specified twelve-minute run from the tread extruder to the drying room and back to the builders, the foreman asked the drivers to take treads directly to the tire builders. The direct runs averaged only two minutes, but

5 *New York Times,* July 7, 1966, p. 15.

the drivers continued to collect pay for twelve. A year and a half later, a time-study man inadvertently discovered the phantom trip time and tried to eliminate it. The drivers "grieved" and won a ruling from the arbitrator that the practice had become, through long practice, a protected work rule, subject to change only with the consent of the union.

Company officials accused the union of protecting featherbedders—but local union officials accused the foremen in the tire-building department of conniving with the drivers.

Most work rules develop gradually, almost imperceptibly, from day to day and month to month. They allow an escape from the impersonality of machine and organization. They reduce the grinding frictions of the industrial process for managers as well as workers and allow adjustments to the tensions and pressures of daily shop life. Once developed, however, rules tend to remain, protecting workers' rights and shop practices.[6]

Management's Stake in Industrial Peace

Management representatives also see the merit of informal discussion of common problems. Even on subjects solely within the area of management prerogatives, management officials learn the value of using the union as a channel of communication with the work force. Increasingly, they are recognizing its ability to help them discover sore spots in the plant and develop corrective action.

Human-relations-conscious supervisors are not unaware of the value of obtaining group agreement before initiating changes in work procedure. Rather than deal with a large number of individuals with diverse points of view, management prefers to sit down with a responsible union leader. He is the spokesman who supposedly represents the unified opinion of the entire work force or who can, subsequent to a negotiating session, sell his opinion to the group. Strong local unions are often seen as guarantees that agreements will be honored. Management learns that it can introduce changes in working conditions with much less friction if it obtains the prior approval of the union. In this way it can initiate action for the union. In effect, management has a stake in a local with leadership strong enough to hold the membership to its decisions.

The Union's Stake in Industrial Peace

In general, union leaders look favorably upon these developments as increased opportunities to provide service for their members. They are anxious

[6] James Kuhn and Ivar Berg, "The Trouble with Labor is Featherbedding," *Columbia University Forum,* Vol. 3, No. 2 (Spring 1960), p. 24.

to expand the scope of collective bargaining. They are equally anxious to demonstrate to the management their *responsibility* and so willingly accept the burden of "selling" the agreement to the rank and file and keeping dissidents in line. By being careful to abide by the terms of the agreements reached, they hope to gain additional prestige and control over working conditions in the plant.

The Expanded Grievance Procedure

In this context, the so-called grievance procedure takes on a new meaning. It is more than a purely negative method of appeal *against* management decisions; it verges on a continuous process of problem solving. Furthermore, the solutions obtained are not always limited by the rigid framework of the contract. With reasonably good labor relations, the grievance procedure can be a creative and positive means whereby the parties translate the dry words of the written document into a living relationship.

In most of the relationships studied, it was almost impossible to ascertain *who* began a so-called grievance or even *when* the case started. Union and management officials, officers and rank and file, workers and foremen—all were in such constant touch with one another that rumors, hints, and questions from all sides played a vital role in collective bargaining.

Thus, the foreman may hint to Bill Jones, the steward, that the company is planning a new type of conveyer system. Questions are immediately raised in Bill's mind and in the minds of the men in his department: will this change the number of jobs available? What will happen to the amount of work we do, the skill required, or the wages received? Bill brings the matter to the attention of his local president, who contacts top management. Then begins a series of conferences which may last for months—until some kind of mutually satisfactory settlement is reached. In such a context, it is irrelevant whether union or management made the initial contact or whether a formal written grievance was ever filed.

This expansion of the grievance procedure results in the union's winning broader control over jobs and new responsibilities. In addition to negotiating basic wages, hours, and working conditions, many officers sign agreements or approve plans that determine selective job rates, work loads, seniority benefits, and seniority rights for individual workers as well as groups.

Even in those situations where management jealously guards its prerogatives to assign work, determine technology, etc., the right of the union to file grievances on the application of these decisions makes it a tacit partner in the final settlement. Indeed, in the eyes of its members, the union shares some of the responsibility for management-initiated changes merely through deciding which grievances are most important and deserve strongest support.

Often a member may say:

> If he [the union president] had been on the ball, he would have stopped this when the company first started putting in the equipment. Now that it is in operation, we have a precedent and nothing can be done.

All of this results in a profound change in the union's role. The function of just *protesting* management decisions is subordinated to some degree of *participation* in making them. On the one hand, the union still presses management to obtain the maximum gains for its membership; on the other hand, it must defend the agreements reached through advance consultation or grievance settlements with the rank and file.

Grievance Procedure as Communications Network

Most discussions of the grievance procedure picture a simple and orderly process. It runs something like this: Bill Smith has a problem. He goes to see his foreman to talk it over (Contact 1, Diagram 1). The foreman fails to give him satisfaction, so he sees his steward (Contact 2). The steward goes to the foreman to discuss the matter further (Contact 3).

Assuming that this is unsuccessful, the grievance is "reduced" to a written statement, a copy of which goes to the chief steward (Contact 4). This official discusses the matter with the department superintendent (Contact 5). If no satisfactory solution is reached at this level, then the matter is brought to the attention of the union grievance committee or the executive committee (Contact 6).

One or more members of the executive committee or the business agent contact the industrial relations department or plant management and a formal conference is held (Contact 7). If Bill's problem is particularly knotty and the parties still cannot reach agreement, it goes, finally, to arbitration (Contact 8). This is the typical procedure outlined by the contract.[7]

If we look at the grievance procedure as the communications process by which workers' problems are discussed and resolved, we see that in most circumstances it is less mechanical than the system outlined above.

Take the situation in Bob Small's plant. Bob has a problem and he talks it over with his foreman (Contact 1, Diagram 2). The foreman tells him that there is nothing he can do, that this kind of matter is decided "higher up." So Bob goes to the department head, who gives him roughly the same answer (Contact 2). He ponders whether he should go directly to the industrial relations office himself. Deciding that discretion is the better part of valor, he

---

[7] For the sake of simplicity, we are omitting the procedural steps that include top corporation officials in multiplant organization. Also, we have ignored the role of the International's staff representatives. In many situations, they play an important part in the grievance procedure long before the case goes to arbitration.

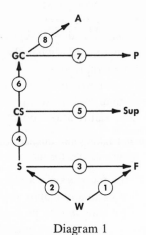

Diagram 1

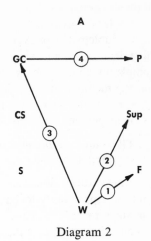

Diagram 2

KEY

W	Worker	**A**	Arbitration
S	Steward	**GC**	Executive committee, grievance committee, business agent, or president
F	Foreman		
CS	Chief steward or grievanceman		
Sup	Superintendent	**P**	Personnel department or production manager

corners the chairman of the grievance committee during the lunch hour (Contact 3). The chairman agrees to discuss this matter informally with the industrial relations manager. Technically, Bob is ignoring the procedure established by the contract. Yet Bob's approach is merely one of a variety of ways by which workers seek redress of their grievances.

Whom Does the Worker Contact?

Of particular interest is the initial step in the grievance process: whom does the worker contact first when he has a complaint? Does he contact the foreman, the steward, or some higher-ranking member of either the union or management? What he does depends to a great extent on the type of union-management relationship in the plant and on the worker's confidence in his foreman and steward. The worker must consider both who has the power to help him and the possibility that he might be penalized if he makes a complaint to the wrong person.

In many companies, before the advent of unionism, the worker was afraid to approach his foreman with a grievance for fear of getting the reputation of being a troublemaker or even of being fired. A grievance procedure is one of the first demands of a newly established union; it permits the orderly handling of complaints and, in theory, eliminates the possibility of reprisal.

But the memory of yesterday is not easily wiped out. Particularly among older workers, this fear of reprisal continues. As one man told us in a plant whose management prides itself on an enlightened industrial relations policy:

> I'll be up for retirement in a few years and I'm not taking any chances of doing anything to endanger that pension. No, sir, no grievances for me.

In "armed truce" situations, both parties compete for the worker's loyalty and for the opportunity to handle his grievances. The company claims that it is anxious to have a chance to settle a worker's problems *before* he sees the union. Thus, if he sees the steward first, the foreman may suspect him of disloyalty to the company (or so the worker fears). Conversely, if stewards are soliciting grievances aggressively, a direct approach to management is considered a slap in the face by the union.

It should be noted that the worker can get the foreman into trouble. Some companies take into account the number of grievances a foreman collects in rating his efficiency. As one top management representative told us:

> The good foreman doesn't have to have grievances. He has enough discretion to be able to settle most complaints—*if* he handles himself well. Many things—for example, pay for overtime work—he is able to adjust if the worker has been wronged. Other things, beyond his scope—for example, where company rules or policies are involved—can be settled if the foreman used tact and diplomacy. There's no question that even where he can't begin action himself, he can settle the fellow's complaint.

In such circumstances, stewards can make effective use of threats to the foreman like the following:

> I've got 13 grievances in my pocket. If you don't wise up, then you get all 13 in the morning. Understand?

The Steward's Role

We have heard union officers say again and again, "The steward is our biggest problem." In theory, stewards are the backbone of the union, the line of communication between officers and members. In spite of this, stewards were hard to recruit in most locals we studied and showed little interest in their job. Frequently, it became almost impossible to fill vacancies, so much so that in one large department only one of 11 steward posts was filled. This was an exceptional case, but most unions have vacancies in their steward rosters.

This holds true even in locals which give stewards a slight financial incentive, by refunding their dues.

A local president explained how "I draft whoever gripes a lot. I get my best men that way." Another took this discouraged attitude:

> You may as well forget that we have any stewards. They're a joke. Even when I appoint them they quit in a month. They don't do much if they stay on. They aren't willing to put the work in, or they are afraid what the company will think. All they do is turn their problems over to us or to their grievanceman.

Of course, the recruitment situation is not always so difficult. In one local election, out of 55 stewardship vacancies, 41 were contested. Even here, however, three of the vacancies were unfilled because no one wanted to run— and a local officer said:

> I'd say that up to half the stewards are just holding down the title. They rely on the chief steward or executive board man to handle their problems for them. Of course, we have a few really good men who can handle themselves well without help. The average one runs to us as soon as he has any problem.

In spite of constitutional provisions, there are no steward elections at all in many locals, either because "it is impossible to get the group to elect anybody, so we must appoint somebody to represent them," or "because a lot of men who get elected are unreliable." In one local, the business agent had to draft candidates. A steward described her "election" as follows:

> After the old steward left, we were without one for three or four months. Then the business agent called a meeting. He wanted me to take the job. I didn't want it. . . . But the business agent told me to take it . . . [later on] I called a meeting to resign, but they wouldn't let me.

Why is the morale of the steward so low? A large part of the reason for this discontent is that his job is changing. In theory, the steward's chief function is that of negotiating with management. As the U.A.W. shop steward guide puts it: "Your post was created because of the workers' need for someone to represent them in dealing with management." In practice, the steward is either by-passed in the grievance procedure or acts as a messenger boy between the rank and file and the officers.

In many instances observed, the typical grievance followed one of two patterns:

1. The worker gets in touch with the most powerful officer available (usually an executive committeeman, although at times a chief steward). This officer gets in touch with the personnel department. Both steward and foreman are by-passed. (See Diagram 3.)

2. Even if the worker tells his problem to the steward, the steward often

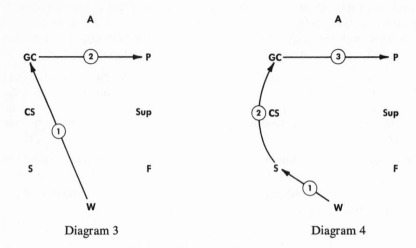

Diagram 3   Diagram 4

hands it over to his chief steward or executive committeeman. One of them contacts the personnel department. The foreman is ignored. (Diagram 4.)

When workers are anxious to obtain swift action, they "shop around" to find the union officer who will "do the most for them." In many plants the foreman possesses little discretion and is largely powerless to make any real adjustment in working conditions. Like the worker himself, he is largely following orders. Consequently, the rank and file realize that bringing a problem to him is an empty formality. And even if the foreman is sympathetic with the workers' problems, he can do very little.

We have observed that foremen sometimes use the grievance procedure as a channel of communications between themselves and top management! Rather than themselves accepting the onus for suggesting changes, they encourage, or at least connive with, the union to bring work problems to the attention of higher management. In many companies, the lowliest steward has readier access to the industrial relations office than does the foreman. A classic example of this comes from a clerical local:

> An assistant department head had been promoted to department head and naturally requested a promotion for his secretary. When his request was rejected, the secretary's chief steward immediately contacted the local president and both made a strong oral protest to the industrial relations manager. Several days later the secretary was upgraded—and the department head thanked the chief steward.

The officers often keep tight control over grievance cases because they are fearful that the stewards may inadvertently establish a precedent unfavorable to the union. In one case, a steward resigned after being reprimanded by a local president for letting a supervisor take over a machine while its operator went to the rest room. The steward claimed that since this technical violation of the contract actually helped the man, there was no harm done. The officers feared this would establish a precedent allowing management to take work away from union members.

However, the officers are concerned lest the stewards be overly militant, giving the impression that the union is breaking its pledged word, as in the case of a steward who took the remarks of a top union official too seriously:

> When this officer asked, "Why the hell should we knock ourselves out when the company feels this way about us?" the steward took this as a signal to call a slow-down. This hot-headed action substantially threatened that local's relationship with management.

For these reasons, the executive board sometimes takes steps to restrict stewards' authority. In one local:

> We agreed that any chairman or committeeman who had a grievance would make absolutely no effort to settle it on the spot, but would immediately get in touch with the business agent. That procedure had a number of rather important effects. One was that they didn't make any snap decisions which would have been colored by their closeness to the situation, and possibly by their lack of training and experience. Another was that they had the advice and critical assistance of someone who stood a little bit out of the immediate picture and wasn't so intimately and personally concerned with the issues at stake.[8]

The stewards themselves are often anxious to transfer grievance responsibility to higher union officers. Many fear recrimination from their foreman. In some situations, top management has accepted collective bargaining in good faith, but lower supervision still handles each grievance as though it were a personal insult. The top officers negotiate directly with staff officers or higher management; the steward must deal with his immediate boss.

Furthermore, the steward is often conscious of the limitations to his bargaining knowledge and ability. In particular, the steward feels handicapped in dealing with complicated technical subjects like job evaluation and time study. Even if he knows the contract backwards and forwards, it is not enough. The written document tells only part of the story. The longer union and management work together, the larger will be the number of informal agreements which interpret the contract.

Few stewards can keep up with these agreements—they do not attend the conferences in which the agreements are evolved, and few locals publish memoranda recording them. Stewards' meetings are usually drab

[8] Andrew H. Whiteford *et al.*, "From Conflict to Cooperation," *Applied Anthropology*, Vol. 5, No. 4 (Fall 1946), p. 12.

affairs in which little important information is communicated. Thus, stewards often find themselves in situations like the following:

> I lost a case that I thought I really had in the bag. I told the foreman that temporary employees could not accumulate seniority. That's what the contract said, plain as day. We fought about it for three months and I was all set to shoot him a written grievance when Bowman [the local president] called me in. He showed me an agreement he signed with the plant manager six months ago which gave those guys their seniority. Was I disgusted!

The Chief Steward

The position of the chief steward (often called a grievanceman or committeeman) has not suffered as greatly as that of the steward, although the situation varies from local to local. In some, his prestige and authority have atrophied as badly as that of the steward; in others, he has direct access to the personnel department and "collects" grievances which might otherwise go to the executive committee or business agent. As in the case of the steward, the strength of the chief steward's position depends to a large extent on whether the members of management with whom he negotiates have the power to conclude agreements.

Even within a single local there may be a significant difference in the way chief stewards play their role. Consider a local president's comments about John Farrell and "Stinky" Mahler:

> John's no better than a lump on a log. He's completely worthless as a chief steward. He's scared to handle a case.
>
> Mahler's one of our most aggressive stewards. He knows how to take a case, to deal with management, and to handle it to the end. We have no trouble from his department.

Four months later the president became frightened of Mahler's growing political power and the fact that men from many departments other than his own were bringing him their problems:

> When I was in the personnel office negotiating, who should walk in but Mahler. You know what a sad excuse he had? I asked, "What do you want, Stinky?" and he said, "Oh, I put a nickel in the Coke machine. The damned thing's out of order and I want my nickel back." Can you imagine that? Expecting us to believe that he'd go to the personnel department just to get a nickel back. This makes a pattern on his part. He's getting bolder and bolder.

The president's chief objection was to Mahler's by-passing of the executive board and contacting of the personnel department directly. To the degree to which chief stewards are capable of dealing with the decision-making levels of management, concentration of power within the hands of the executive board is reduced.

Since chief stewards rarely deal solely with their *immediate* supervisors, the strength of their position relative to that of stewards is greater. They negotiate with men in the "office" as well as men in the "shop" and thus feel freer from possible retribution.

Chief stewards are often anxious to increase their power. Many of the shrewder ones build alliances with local officers. A local vice-president remarked:

> A good chief steward will always call you down to help settle the case. He knows it means votes for you and you can do something for him in return.

Some chief stewards are glad to get assistance from more experienced officers, who in turn will share some of the responsibility if the grievance "turns sour." On the other hand, there are those who want a free hand to handle their own problems and who resent the unwanted intrusion of top union officers. Bill Henry resigned over this issue:

> Bill was one of the few men in his department interested in the union. For over six years he had served as chief steward and given much of his spare time to the cause.
>
> The department had been plagued by a series of internal grievances and Bill's decisions were not always popular. Recently, he was able to get the contending parties in a particularly difficult seniority dispute to come more or less to an agreement. Several days ago, one disaffected individual approached the local president, who without consulting Bill, completely reversed him. Immediately there was a new epidemic of grievances. Bill felt there was nothing left to do but resign.

Such conflicts between chief stewards and officers are most acute at election time—as are disputes between the officers themselves.

Union or Management Initiative?

Of course, not all grievances are initiated by individual workers—some relate to entire departments and, in these cases, the chief steward takes the responsibility of bringing the problem to management's attention. Still other grievances may affect a large number of workers, although no single worker feels strongly enough to register a complaint. In one plant, for example, an executive board member noted that one of the major entrances to the plant was locked during the period between shift changes. During a lull in one of the executive committee meetings, he suggested that this violated a state law and endangered the safety of the men in the plant. "And they can't treat us like animals in a pen!" The next week the bargaining committee presented their case to the head of the personnel department.

Often management initiates the action. Many stewards said, "Whenever there is a vacancy coming up, the foreman lets me know and we sit down to decide who fills it."

Thus, there are numerous channels which can be used in grievance negotiations. Indeed, it may be that the term *grievance* itself is confusing and instead the whole process should be considered as one of *problem-solving*.

Certainly our experiences suggest that one of the prime indicators of good labor-management relations is that discussion of problems is initiated by management almost as often as by the union. For instance, the foreman may discuss a disciplinary problem with the steward before taking action—rather than waiting for a grievance to be filed after he takes action.

Except in "armed truce" situations, where the union officers are anxious to harass management with the maximum number of grievances, there is a general reluctance to reduce important grievances to writing.

The rank-and-file worker fears that signing his name to a complaint is "sticking his neck out" and may make him look like a "troublemaker." Stewards and higher officers have learned that their freedom to make adjustments is much greater when they can deal with management informally—without the necessity of pointing to a particular clause in the contract and proving that it was violated.

For these reasons, grievances are reduced to writing only after other means have failed. Sometimes this happens when a rank-and-file group feels that the officers are not acting promptly on its grievances. At times, too, when the top officers themselves have failed in their efforts at informal negotiations, they may institute the formal machinery as a means of exerting further pressure on management and perhaps preparing the way for possible arbitration. In such cases, the local president often helps the steward word his grievance, while the foreman's reply is usually cleared with his supervisor. In fact, the foreman's answer is usually a verbatim record of what higher management had said earlier—informally.

Conclusion

The flexible nature of the *real* grievance procedure (as distinct from that outlined by the contract) encourages a general tendency to "by-pass" the steward and deprive him of his position as the first-line bargaining agent. In most of the cases observed, negotiations with management were handled by a few individuals—perhaps as few as two or three in plants employing 500 to 1,000 —and by a proportionately larger number in the bigger plants. Not only is the steward by-passed in a formal sense, but in many cases he is not included in the mainstream of union intelligence. In addition to his being deprived of the opportunity to participate in the settlement of grievances concerning his own department, in many cases such settlements are made entirely without his knowledge. No wonder his morale is low!

In most newly organized plants the steward performs two very important functions: recruiting new members and collecting dues. However, many plants have a union shop and, in many of those which do not, almost 100 per cent of the workers belong to the union. Furthermore, the checkoff system, which is more and more widely adopted, eliminates the necessity of individual dues collections. Under these circumstances, of the union-building functions only the nasty jobs are left—such as selling dance tickets and raffle chances.

As long as union-management relations remain in a state of constant conflict the steward performs an important function. He is encouraged to collect grievances, start wildcat strikes, and prod the workers into harassing management in every possible way. Thus, the decline of the steward is in part a function of improving labor-management relations.

Still, the steward's decline should not be overemphasized. Many stewards still serve as lines of communication between their departments and the local executive board. Even though they do not negotiate grievances, they provide valuable assistance to the officers. In some situations, there is an implicit exchange of favors—the officers will give top priority to the steward's grievance in return for which he provides them with political support. In other cases, as we shall see, the steward is able to mobilize self-help techniques and negotiate directly with management—often doing so in direct opposition to the local-wide officers.

This chapter has emphasized the flexible nature of the grievance procedure as it exists in the plants we observed. The next chapter will take up the fact that grievances often involve a conflict between various groups within the union.

Subsequent chapters deal with repercussions on *internal* union relations as *external* labor-management relations move toward industrial peace. We seek to show the types of internal adjustments which locals must make in order to adapt to a long period of regulated struggle. Among the problems are these:

1. The tendency of the steward's function to diminish (This occurs because the increasing technicality of the subjects handled and the informal nature of the grievance procedure result in a concentration of bargaining in the hands of top local officers and their counterparts on the management side.)

2. The union's need to choose between the conflicting demands of individuals and groups in matters such as seniority (Here, settlements within its own ranks must precede bargaining with management.)

3. The transfer to the local and its officers of some of the aggressions formerly directed against management (This occurs as the local increasingly performs quasi-supervisory functions.)

These then, may provide one explanation (although there are others) for the falling off of interest and participation noted in many unions.

3

Conflicting Interest Groups

A union can be looked at in two ways; as a unified body of members promoting the common welfare through collective action, and as a confederation of competing interest groups, each with individual goals. This chapter emphasizes the second aspect—the elements of difference between groups within the local, rather than the deceptive unity presented to outsiders. (This emphasis gives us a one-sided picture: Unionism could never have reached its present strength unless union members were united on essentials.)

Even though disguised by the industrial union structure, the elements of conflict are less obvious than in the jurisdictional disputes between craft unions, but just as real. For example, the same factor of job scarcity which motivates the craft union can operate within the plant-wide local.

The worker in the plant is not only a company employee and a union member, but also a member of countless other special-interest groups; he may be a mill operator on the night shift, he may have low seniority, he may be paid on an "incentive rate," and so forth. Where shared by others, each of these aspects of his status can be the basis of a special-interest group, the members of which may have bargaining objectives that conflict with those of union "brothers."

Difficult adjustments must be made *internally* during the course of the union's *external* negotiations with management. What may appear to management as a common union policy is often the resultant of numerous compromises among divergent interest groups within the rank and file.

Areas of Conflict

In an active local, the union officers have demands made upon them in an almost continuous stream. The rank and file constantly bring them problems on which they want the union to take immediate action. These demands can be divided into three classes: (1) those on which the union and its members can be reasonably united against the company, such as grievances against company-imposed discipline or demands for general wage increases; (2) those through which some groups may benefit a great deal but others only slightly, if at all. (For example, a request for increased nightwork differentials is of immediate importance only to workers on extra shifts. Since the union's bargaining power is limited, as is management's ability to pay, greater gains by one group will often be counterbalanced by lesser gains by others.); and (3) those through which one group can gain only at the direct expense of some other individual or group. (Typical of these are seniority questions. For example, one worker may be able to win a promotion only through taking the opportunity away from another.)

Any of these problems may arise either in the form of a grievance under the existing contract or as a demand for new and changed contract clauses during negotiations. In form, at least, they are directed against management. However, before the union can begin to "process" these demands it must make up its own mind just what to ask for. This often involves politically difficult decisions.

Where Groups Generally Agree

Traditionally, in discussions of labor relations, the emphasis has been placed on the first class of problem. Even here the union's bargaining position is limited, and sometimes a choice must be made between conflicting goals of interest groups. For instance, in asking for a general wage increase, officers must often choose between asking for the increase in "cents-per-hour" (as favored by the lower-paid groups) or "percentage-wise" (as the higher paid would like). Again, it would seem that no one on the union's side would be hurt if Bill Smith's disciplinary layoff could be successfully challenged. However, many members object to "another guy's getting away with murder." This is particularly true if the offense in question involves other individuals, such as fighting or "laying down on the job" when a team operation is involved.

In any case, the union still cannot win every grievance. If it wins Smith's, it may do so at the expense of losing Jones's. The settlement of grievance cases often involves logrolling with management. One case may be traded off to win another. Even arbitration involves a choice. No union can afford (politically or economically) to arbitrate everything—and if it could, an intergroup dispute might arise between those whose cases involve arbitration and those who pay the arbitration costs. Since this type of problem is well known, our attention will be concentrated on the other two classes of problem.

Where One Group Gains Relatively More Than Another

By now it is generally accepted that, as a cause of worker dissatisfaction, differences between wage rates are almost as important as their absolute levels.

> Wage differentials are a mark of social status in the factory organization. If they do not correspond with the relative significance of jobs, as employees view them, the workers' sense of justice is outraged.[1]

Whenever the union officers obtain improved earnings for one group, they reduce the relative prestige of other workers. The elimination of what are inequities in the eyes of one group may create inequities in the eyes of a competing department.

A typical example comes from a clerical local. Management told the girls in a large office to go home at midday because there was insufficient work for them. They complained to the union, which eventually won them a full day's pay. Immediately, a flood of abuse was poured on the officers by the girls who had actually worked the entire period for the same pay.

A more complicated case concerns an industrial union which won unusually "loose" incentive rates for "labor pool" jobs.[2] As a result, unskilled men obtained earnings nearly double those of skilled workers in the same plant. These skilled workers felt embarrassed when weekly paychecks were compared in the shop and outside the plant. Realizing that under the contract they had no chance of increasing their own earnings, they insisted that the union try to "tighten" the incentive rates of the labor pool. Of course, the men in the "pool" argued that their higher earnings were entirely the result of hard work rather than faulty rate setting. Union leaders were in a quandary. If they were a party to reducing the earnings of the men in the labor pool, they would be accused of playing management's game. On the

---

[1] Pigors and Myers, *Personnel Administration* (2nd ed. New York: McGraw-Hill Book Co., 1951), p. 255.

[2] "Loose" incentive rates are those which are particularly lucrative. "Labor pool" jobs are those at the bottom of the plant promotional ladder. For a more extensive discussion of these incentive problems see Leonard R. Sayles, "The Impact of Incentives on Inter-Group Work Relations," *Personnel,* Vol. 28, No. 6 (May, 1952), pp. 483–490.

other hand, the skilled dayworkers were protesting that the union was "just run for the benefit of those unskilled pieceworkers."

Whenever the union initiates or acquiesces to change affecting job evaluation or incentive rates, it runs the risk of upsetting *customary differentials.* When the men "bid" for one job rather than another, they do so in the expectation that the wages paid on these jobs will maintain their relative positions. When this balance is upset—for example, by a new job-evaluation plan that substantially increases the rates for some jobs—some men will feel that their expectations have been unjustly thwarted.

In situations like this, management can afford to be neutral. Often the contract sets aside one lump sum to cover inequities. When this happens, one group can get an increase only at the expense of another.

The "rate buster" provides an equally difficult problem.[3] Individuals or entire groups who produce too much can be extremely embarrassing to the union.

Such a problem arose during the establishment of an incentive system. The management concerned was moving slowly and with great care. The joiner's "rates" were the first to be set. At the beginning, these were temporary; then after a two-year trial they were made permanent. During the testing period, the men kept production down so that the rates ultimately set would be low. After the rates were established, they increased their output (and earnings) almost daily. But other men in the same department, who expected that an incentive plan would soon be developed for their jobs too, complained that this group's high production was spoiling things: the company would never again believe the trial period results, and the new rates, it was feared, would be mercilessly low. As a consequence, they asked the union to put pressure on the group to "take it easy." Naturally the men involved felt that after making sacrifices for two years they deserved a little "gravy." In this case, the local officers had to decide whether to exert pressure and risk antagonizing this group or to endanger future incentive rates.

The two cases described above illustrate how the introduction of an incentive plan can disrupt the harmony within a local. Similar conflicts can arise between incentive workers and the hourly-rate men who service them. This relationship is always delicate, but particularly so when the amount of work done by one group is a function of that done by another. If the dayworkers slow down, the incentive group feels deprived of its opportunity to earn money. But if the incentive workers speed up, those on day rates feel that they are doing something for nothing since their earnings remain constant.

In a recent strike, an entire plant was shut down to support the demands of

[3] A "rate buster" is a worker who produces more than the standard informally agreed on by his group. Cf. Melville Dalton, "The Industrial Rate Buster: A Characterization," *Applied Anthropology,* Vol. 7, No. 7 (Winter 1948), pp. 5–18.

Department X for a more liberal incentive plan. Once the plan was granted, the department greatly increased its production—much to the disgust of the dayworkers in Department Y, the next step in the production line. They complained that they had sacrificed two weeks' pay during the strike only to find that their own work load had increased without extra compensation.

Thus, one group's winning of a grievance may hurt other groups in a variety of ways.

Where One Group Gains at the Direct Expense of Another

Many of the decisions which union officers must make involve more than a relative loss by some group within the rank and file. In many cases, there is a strong possibility that some members will be hurt as much as others are benefited. Thus, from the point of view of the membership as a whole, there can be no real victory even though the union's institutional power vis-à-vis the management may be enhanced.

A simple example illustrates this point. The grinding and cutting departments in a large manufacturing plant can perform roughly the same operations. When business declined the grinders presented a grievance because their work was being transferred to the cutters, resulting in layoffs for their own department. The officers were faced with a dilemma. If they pursued the grievance, they would penalize one group; if they did not, they would hurt the other.

The division of retroactive pay often introduces similar problems. In a typical situation, an old contract expired on July 30 and the parties agreed that any wage increase would be retroactive to that date. Final agreement on a 10-cents-an-hour increase was reached November 16. It was estimated that the average worker would receive about $70 in back pay, although those with a great deal of overtime would get much more. Rather than go through the heavy expense of computing the amount owed each worker separately, the company proposed to give a lump-sum bonus of $85. Approximately 85 per cent of the workers would gain by this—but the 15 per cent minority really "raised the roof" at a meeting called to ratify the contract. Problems like this often lead to litigation.

Specific Problems

Seniority

Seniority disputes are the cause of many internal union conflicts. Increasingly, seniority is becoming the worker's primary guarantee of economic security. Whether a man wins a promotion or is laid off, whether he is downgraded or put on the night shift—all these, and many other aspects of a worker's job and earnings—depend on this one important factor.

Yet, as the cases described below illustrate, the determination of who is the "senior man" in a given case may involve an arbitrary judgment. Often these decisions are extremely complex, and the contract provides an unsatisfactory guide to the "right" decisions.

A typical problem started when a lift truck which had been servicing Department A began to be used in Department B. After a time, the drivers of the lift truck were instructed to report to the foreman of Department B. Soon the men in Department B claimed that the job belonged to them and that the men in Department A should return to their own department.

In plants where work is scheduled unevenly and layoffs are common, "bumping," or displacing from his job the man with lower seniority, is the normal practice. Men in every department fear that when cutbacks occur they will lose their jobs to those with higher seniority. Under these circumstances, the arrangement of the so-called "job progression" ladders is extremely important. Men in each occupational group want to maximize the number of jobs below them, into which they can bump in case of a cutback in employment. By the same token, they want to minimize the number of men who can bump them from above.

Many departments openly compete to have low-seniority groups placed below *them* in the promotional ladder. As a result, some groups whose members have relatively high seniority are orphaned. They have no job beneath them into which they can bump.

Union shop committees often have the unpleasant task of mediating these disputes. Some locals have tried to avoid the problem by providing that the decisions should be made by the departments directly concerned. This attempt is usually ineffective since the minority will almost always complain to the union that the majority decision was unfair. Usually, at some point the union officers find themselves placed in the position of having to say that one group was right and the other was wrong.

Of course, management does have its own interest in this problem. Continuous shifting of jobs is not conducive to morale and productivity. Filling of jobs by inexperienced or partially trained workers is expensive. For these reasons, too, rapid shifting of personnel is often opposed. However, within broad limits, management may not care whom the union ultimately declares to be the "senior man."

The principle that "seniority shall prevail" merely states the problem. Seniority is not a rigid measuring rod, but a flexible one. It is subject to the use of each group in the pursuance of its own interests.

Thus seniority provides a difficult internal union problem. The uninitiated observer is always surprised at the tremendous proportion of grievances and intergroup disputes which revolve around this one issue. In the unions we have studied, decisions affecting promotions, demotions, layoffs, transfers, and shift preference easily consume one-third of the time of union officers. In each of these areas, a decision which helps one union member is usually going to hurt another. The resulting pressures on the officers are enormous.

Level of Employment

Whenever output is curtailed, the union and management are faced with two alternatives: reducing the workweek or laying off the less senior employees. Of course, the employer may have preferences of his own, but the union, too, must decide what it wants. This is particularly a problem at the time the contract is being negotiated. Should short-service employees have the opportunity to participate in work-sharing or should they be laid off to make more work for the longer-service members; and what is the dividing line between the two groups?

The opposite problem arises when production expands. In one such situation, the top paid employees demanded overtime (meaning the right to work extra hours at premium rates), while those who held jobs lower on the promotional ladder insisted that they be promoted to the higher grade and new employees hired to fill in at the bottom.

The cases described above illustrate the areas in which group conflicts can arise and the types of problems these present to the union leadership. When the uninformed observer considers worker demands for changes in wages, problems of incentive rate setting, and disputes over layoffs and promotions, he does not ordinarily consider these as possible areas of intergroup conflict. Yet, in each of these cases, the union must reconcile its internal differences before it can present a united front to management.

There is the additional complication that, in many cases, the local leadership has made prior agreements, formal or informal, with management. These commit the union to a specific policy or course of action—for example, that certain work should be done by the splicers rather than the joiners. But if the joiners file a grievance against this, their grievance is, in fact, directed just as much against the union as against the company. For if the union is to give in to the joiners, it must break its implicit agreement with the splicers and management. Most leaders appear anxious to seem responsible. They prefer not to break their word with the company. If they do, it will jeopardize their "informal relations" and make it increasingly difficult to obtain other agreements in the future.

Dynamics of Intergroup Conflicts

The previous section has shown the types of problems which lead to intergroup conflict. This section will deal with the dynamics of these conflicts—

how they arise and the types of weapons used by the opposing parties to gain their ends.

The Case of the Spinners   As an introduction, it may be valuable to trace the history of a single case, showing how the groups involved compared their earnings and working conditions, how this affected plant life and normal work relations, and how these work groups used a broad range of techniques to further their ends.

In a large manufacturing plant, a conflict arose between the men who operated the new spinning machines and those who operated the old ones. The old "standard" spinning machines were operated chiefly by high-seniority men, who were paid an hourly rate. For nine years the company had been experimenting with new machines which were faster and easier to run. During this period they had been operated by younger men with low seniority. After a two-year tryout of the new machines, their operators were placed on incentive rates.

To obtain the union's approval, management granted a "loose" rate (one on which it is easy to obtain high earnings). The union readily accepted, believing that unless the long-run productivity of this particular department was improved, the company would move its operations to another plant.

However, the old spinners, who were politically powerful in the union, resented the incentive system. They feared it would establish a precedent for working too fast and perhaps even reduce the amount of work available to them. Eventually, this could mean fewer jobs.

Even before the incentive plan was accepted, the men on the old spinners derided the younger men as "damn fools for working themselves to death." In turn, the younger men were resentful of the old spinners' "creamy jobs" and were upset that the seniority system forced them to take what was then less desirable work, with little chance of obtaining jobs on the old machines.

However, after the plan was in effect, the men started comparing paychecks in neighborhood bars. It became obvious that the younger men, on incentive, were earning a great deal more than the older spinners on their hourly rate. Since the two types of machines had adjacent locations, the old spinners were able to watch the ever-increasing production on the other line. With growing anxiety, they saw the differentials between their earnings becoming larger.

The two lines had never been friendly. Now they began to exchange angry threats. Several top-seniority spinners told the "youngsters":

> You guys better save what you are earning because you're not going to be on these jobs very long. We're coming over to take them. They're ours because we're the oldest men in the department.

To be sure, some of this was in jest, but the serious undertone prompted a group of the youngest, who had nothing to lose, to tell off their adversaries:

> Don't start anything because if you try to bump us [use the seniority pro-
> visions of the contract to take their jobs] we're going to fix these jobs so no
> one wants them.

The reply of hourly-rate spinners was in terms of their right to the job, as
older, senior employees in the department:

> Why should some young guy that has been in the plant less than a year
> be taking home 30 dollars more a week than guys like us that have been
> here more than 15 years? We'll be the laughing stock of the plant.

The new spinners were just as self-righteous:

> We took these jobs when no one else wanted them. We stuck to them
> through two years of a trial period when everyone else was laughing at us,
> and you fellows have no right to come over and bump us off.

The old spinners first tried to pressure their stewards and grievancemen
into taking some action. Some informally contacted the local president and
the International representative in order to get their opinion on whether it
would be legal for them to bump onto the new machines. When no reply was
received, three of the more vocal old spinners wrote out a formal grievance to
their steward outlining their right to the new job and demanding that the
union do something about the threat of the youngsters to use production
increases to "ruin the new job."

In the meantime, the incentive workers made good their threat to accelerate their production increases, hoping thereby to discourage the older men
from any further interest in the job. Their logic was this: if they worked very
hard, management would expect much more production than the older men,
who had been "spoiled" on an hourly-rated job, would be willing to put out.

The older men responded by calling a departmental meeting as authorized
by the union constitution. Although this was boycotted by the majority of the
new spinners, there was still spirited discussion. The result was obvious from
the start—a motion was passed to "clarify the seniority provisions of the
contract" by authorizing bumping.

The younger men heard the results the next day. They, too, submitted a
formal grievance in writing, enunciating their claims to the incentive jobs.
This was based on the promises of the local president and the chairman of
the grievance committee that anyone who completed the trial period would
gain seniority on the job.

To summarize, in order to get acceptance of technological change, the
company offered unusually high earnings for one job. This changed its at-
tractiveness relative to other jobs—and thus upset the social structure of the
shop. The senior employees felt that their prestige and earnings were threatened. As a means of defense, they utilized the grievance procedure and departmental meetings. In return, the younger workers resorted to self-help

measures (a speedup!). (This provided an issue in the next election.) It is cases of this complexity which plague the life of the union official.

Increasing Importance of the Differences

Before the union was organized, poor communications made it difficult for one group to compare itself with another. Information about weekly paychecks, hours worked, seniority, and all the rest could be passed from group to group only by means of rumors and personal friendships.

The unions have opened new channels of communication. Contract requirements that seniority lists and job vacancies be posted create a wealth of opportunities for workers to compare their positions in the plant. Job evaluation rates all the jobs in the plant against *each other*. Union participation in incentive rate setting results in publicity for many elements which the average worker never before considered important or felt he could understand. Just as workers are now sensitive to cost-of-living indices, they know what the "other guys are getting and how hard they work for it."

Increasingly, over-all working conditions are determined through company-wide or industry-wide negotiations. As a result, a worker as an individual can do little about his basic wage rate, but when he notices that the man next to him is obtaining more than his fair share of overtime he can complain —with at least a fair chance of success.

The grievance procedure provides an orderly channel through which pressure can be exerted upon management. Furthermore, to some extent the union is a forum, within which efforts can be made to reconcile differences between groups.

Earlier chapters have shown how "industrial peace" and "working harmony" result in the union's winning additional bargaining rights in areas which were once solely management's prerogative. However, many of these added areas of responsibility are also areas where intergroup differences may arise. The relative strength of the union is often correlated with its success in expanding the scope of collective bargaining. This, too, may give rise to internal differences which can split the union unless the officers show human-relations statesmanship of the highest order.

Passing the problem to management, logical argument, even a majority vote of the members involved—all often fail to relieve the officers of the necessity for making a politically difficult decision. In considering a grievance, the local leadership must take into account, first, how it affects the relationship with management, second, what it does to the balance between competing groups in the plant community and, third, various types of pressures the rival groups will be able to exert. These pressures are the subject of the next chapter.

4

Group Pressures upon
Union Officers

Most union members realize that their complaints must compete with those from other work groups. Rather than sit idly by while their grievances are being considered, interested work groups make use of a battery of weapons to expedite the process. Sometimes these are directed against the company, sometimes against rival work groups. In most cases, they are exerted directly on the union officers to induce them to pressure management.

The range of weapons varies from the "primitive" self-help techniques available even to unorganized workers, through short-term pressures aimed at getting the officers to handle immediate problems, to longer-run efforts directed at increasing the political power of the group within the union.

Unorganized workers are not completely without bargaining power. In fact, they have available to them all the weapons used by the union. The difference made by unionism is that of coordination and outside support. Both organized and unorganized workers can express their dissatisfaction through absenteeism, quitting, or requesting transfers. More forceful and concerted measures are available when unorganized workers act as a group. Among these are slowdowns, sit-down strikes, wildcat walkouts, and even acts of direct sabotage. These are primitive weapons; but as we shall see, even organized workers use them when they feel their officers are not paying sufficient attention to their just complaints.

Unionism provides a less violent way of expressing group dissatisfaction— the grievance procedure. Yet, a grievance has many hurdles to jump before the alleged inequity is corrected. These hurdles may arise from the desires of the officers to conserve limited bargaining power and from opposition by other groups whose interests would be hurt if the grievance proved to be successful.

It takes months, even years, before some grievances are resolved. In order to accelerate favorable action, members can resort to the following: (1) pressures within the framework of the grievance procedure, such as "button-holing" officers and making appeals at membership meetings; (2) action designed to improve their own long-run political position, such as voting for officers likely to favor their cause; and (3) self-help techniques, such as slow-downs and wildcat strikes—primitive tactics also available to the unorganized group.

Pressures within the Grievance Procedure

When a group feels that its just demands are being stalled or sidetracked, it first takes steps to expedite the grievance procedure by putting pressure upon some officers and, often, by ignoring others.

Not all officers will be equally sympathetic to the members' complaints. But the workers "shop around," and if one officer turns them down, they try to find someone more cooperative.

In many cases, the officer most frequently appealed to is the president or the chairman of the grievance committee—or even a strong secretary or vice-president. Such officers gain political advantage by successfully processing grievances. Even when they know they cannot be successful they learn how to avoid giving a direct "no," how to pass the buck to the company, to other officers, or— as is always convenient—to the International.

The rank and file take advantage of the officers' anxiety to please. If they feel that a given officer is not being assiduous enough they can always accuse him of "spelling out," of looking after the interests of management rather than those of the union. Thus the ability to shop around provides effective leverage for influencing the leadership.

No leader who wants to stay in office would dare restrict his calling hours to the time he spends at the union office or at grievance meetings. He finds no sanctuary in his home, particularly if he has a telephone:

> When I'm away, my daughter takes ten to fifteen calls and makes notes on them. Why, I get calls at two or three in the morning. The night shift thinks that since they are working, I ought to be too.

Some leaders have their telephones removed; others have unlisted numbers. But in the shop the union officer is subject to the acid test:

> If you really want to see some grievances, you ought to be around on Friday. Boy, I think this next Friday I'm going to be out of town, visiting my grandmother in Ohio. The minute they see their paychecks, they're out for you. In the morning, I go for a cup of coffee, it sometimes takes me two hours to get out of the lunchroom. There are a whole line of people waiting to see you, bringing up this case or that one.

Groups which find such informal techniques unsuccessful in prodding the officers to action can bring their problem to the attention of the local membership meeting. An orderly way of doing this is to introduce a formal resolution directing the leadership to take specific action in their case. Such an approach is not common. It is much more likely that someone will simply get up and ask the president or business agent point-blank:

> When are we going to get action on our overtime pay? We've had our claim in for three months and you guys are still sitting on your fat rear ends!

A more demonstrative note is struck when the speaker comes armed with a lengthy petition, signed by an entire department.

Department meetings provide another means of exerting pressure on the officers. Although the officers usually look upon these meetings as a means of obtaining ratification for supplemental agreements affecting only one department, they often get out of hand when the rank-and-file members convert them into gripe sessions.

Parliamentary rules of decorum prevent the members from being too violent at regular meetings, but there are no holds barred when the department meets alone. In local-wide meetings, the officers can limit the discussion to matters affecting "general welfare"; the department meetings get down to specific cases and personalities. The members have the officers on the spot and make the most of it. At times, the meeting can degenerate into an inquisition ending in an uproar as charges of "sellout" and "company man" abound.

Improving Their Long-run Political Position

The kinds of pressures discussed so far might well be called *short run;* they are useful in expediting specific grievances of individuals or groups. However, many groups are intent on improving their longer-run chances of exerting effective control over the actions of their leaders. To do this, it is necessary to gain political strength through some form of direct *participation* in union affairs.

A single key officer can provide more help than a large bloc of members who merely attend meetings. Any department is frank to admit that it has gained or could profit by electing one of its number as local president or chief steward. As one recalled: "Things haven't been the same for us since Joe Corse [a former president] left the plant."

This advantage often leads to fierce competition between departments, particularly in chief stewards' elections. Although the steward is losing some of his power, it is still important to have the right man as a communications link with the top union officers and management. The man who holds the title of steward is able to say things which would be foolhardy for the average member. Furthermore, unless a steward backs it up, a grievance may have "rough sledding" when it reaches the higher stages of the negotiations process. Few rank-and-file members are likely to assume the role of the go-between. One department, that admitted its steward was just a "messenger boy," still used him as its spokesman in dealing with outside groups.

Self-help Techniques

If the use of the normal channel of the grievance procedure or of participation in union affairs does not produce the better working conditions desired, the group may revert to the "primitive" self-help techniques discussed above. Of course, union leaders themselves at times make use of sit-downs, slowdowns, and mass absenteeism as a means of exerting pressure on management. In most cases, they refuse to accept public responsibility for "spontaneous action"—but it often serves their purpose. However, it would be a mistake to assume that this is always true.

Often these self-help techniques are extremely embarrassing to the officers' efforts to appear responsible. The network of informal relations which enable union officers to achieve advantageous settlement of grievances, even when these are not fully justified by the contract, are based on the officers' ability to provide unimpeded production as a *quid pro quo*. If the officers are unable to do this, their bargaining power is greatly diminished. Indeed, management officials may begin to bargain directly with the complainants themselves.

In rare instances, self-help techniques are utilized in battles for political control of great Internationals. More commonly, they are used for more limited objectives, such as a "looser" incentive rate or a change in the promotional ladder. Here, pressure is exerted more or less indiscriminately against officials of both union and management, although, as the spinners' case pointed out, such pressures can also operate against a rival work group.

Students of industrial relations are well aware of workers' ability to restrict or control output. Standards of output seem almost uniform in industry, regardless of whether workers are paid on incentive or day rate. Furthermore, these standards are flexible—the "right" level of production can easily be manipulated to meet new conditions, and tremendous pressures can be placed upon group members who do not respond appropriately.

Given a situation where union leaders desire to build a reputation for responsibility, production control is an effective force in the hands of dissatisfied work groups. One worker told how:

> We were corkscrewing production a little bit, taking it up and taking it down. Often it went down below the day rate. The whole thing is, most of the fellows believe that the regular grievance machinery is too darn slow. The company keeps telling us that our case has to wait until they handle a whole lot of others, so we wanted to put some pressure on them to hurry things up. We want to short-circuit it really. The fellows want some immediate action. They figure that the way to do it is to cut down on production.

This places officers in a dilemma. If they permit rank-and-file members to be punished for their militancy they will be subject to charges of "sellout." On the other hand, if they take a firm stand against management they will lose all chance for building good relations. Often the officers adopt a compromise solution. They persuade the workers to cease their self-help activity, in return for which they promise that their grievances will be pushed with greater energy. In this manner, both company and union officials are pressed to work harder when the men begin taking matters into their own hands.

Another self-help technique involves threats to leave a union or to form or join another. Where there is no union shop, a group may threaten to resign en masse, and even where there is a union shop, gestures toward inviting competing Internationals to enter the situation may strike fear into the hearts of the officers. Thus one of a group of angry cranemen threatened:

> We should have gotten out of this union a long time ago and organized our own. After all, we are pretty skilled around here, and if we walk off our jobs, no one can work. This way we're just a few men in this local and don't have a voice. But if we had our separate local, they would listen to us.

Such coercion is often successful; in this case the men won seniority rights to a newly created job.

Although the officers are often intimidated by the coercive techniques applied by strongly united groups, they come to rely on the solidarity of those groups when bargaining with management. Such support is important in convincing management that changes are imperative.

Many officers have had disillusioning experiences when departments with grievances failed to back up their demands by the appropriate action. Most of these departments are divided internally. Having no real internal leadership, and disagreeing on what they should fight for, their outbursts of indignation against either union or management are not rationally directed. When the break comes it is frequently a wildcat walkout (without warning to the union), with many frustrations spilling out over a single unsettled griev-ance. To management, as well as to the union, it will appear that the men are overreacting to a relatively unimportant issue.

Conclusion

The groups have a battery of weapons at their disposal. For greatest effec-tiveness they do not use one technique to the exclusion of others. When the grievance procedure fails, they may resort to self-help or political activity within the union. No single form of pressure is necessarily followed to its logical end. Departments jump from one form of activity to another—slowing down production, filing grievances, requesting transfers, making threats at union meetings, and all the rest.

When the officers are committed to industrial peace, self-help techniques which impede production embarrass the union officers as well as manage-ment. Indeed, the very desire of these officers to maintain harmonious rela-tions with top management may sometimes encourage "primitive" direct action within the shop. The question of how the officers react to these pres-sures is discussed in the next chapter.

5

Reaction of Pressures and Evaluation of Grievances

All the pressures described in the previous chapter come to bear on the local officers at one point or another in the grievance procedure. In responding to the demands made upon them, the officers must develop some system of priority. Many grievances are contradictory (particularly where there are conflicting group interests), some are unjustified, and all require time, energy, and the expenditure of the union's limited bargaining power. Only a few will have strategic importance to the union as a whole.

Before deciding what to do with a grievance, the officers must consider its possible ramifications upon (1) political relationships within the local itself, (2) the union's relationship with management, and (3) the amount of support the members will provide in pushing the case. These will be discussed in turn.

Frequently, the officers must assign a low priority to a grievance even though it has the enthusiastic support of a substantial number of interested members. To insulate themselves against rank-and-file pressure, and to provide an orderly system for the consideration of all grievances, the officers have adopted certain techniques which increase their control over the whole day-to-day bargaining process. Without these contrivances, the operations of the grievance procedure could generate a fatal political backlash that might thrust the existing leadership from office.

Political Effect

How an officer handles a case has important effects on his own political position and on the bargaining power of the union. Of course, if he obviously mismanages the grievance, it will soon be known all over the plant. But more is involved.

What seems like a simple grievance often has repercussions that outweigh its superficial importance. In dealing with any grievance, the officers try to take into account the vested interests of all groups that may be affected. Furthermore, the officers realize that in pushing a grievance supported by a few individuals they may dissipate the bargaining power of the entire group. Consider the following case:

> Several machine operators were convinced that their job duties had changed sufficiently to warrant a pay increase. Since management was having difficulty in recruiting machine operators, it probably would have granted the increase without too much pressure. Although the union admitted the justice of the case, the officers were reluctant to push for a settlement, fearing that this would "take the pressure off" the company to grant a general wage increase for the entire department.

Most leaders are aware that the pros and cons of particular grievances are discussed at length within the shop. Opinions diverge radically as to which grievances should be pushed. As one leader described the problem: "The minute the word leaks out that there is a grievance, there are three hundred shop lawyers telling you what to do."

It is often difficult to determine whether a grievance is the result of a single "agitator" or really has attracted widespread emotional interest on the part of the rank and file.

The winning of one grievance often provides an obvious incentive for others to try the same thing. As one leader put it, "As soon as one man wins a spot increase, you have everybody trying to get the same thing, you're flooded with grievances you can't win."

Maintaining Relations with Management

The average union leader is almost as concerned about maintaining good relations with management as he is with obtaining rank-and-file support. Management and union officials who administer the contract have to deal with each other every day. If the officers press complaints that appear unwarranted, ridiculous, or petty they run the risk of antagonizing the company and looking silly in the process. The union officer's ability to obtain important concessions from the company depends to some extent upon his personal relationship with management.

The shrewd union negotiator knows that if he pushes one grievance he may jeopardize his later chances of success; in addition, he would like to avoid clogging the grievance machinery with an excessive number of cases. Instead of pushing them all with equal determination, he would prefer to be selective, avoiding the areas of strongest management resistance; by sidetracking some problems, he can get quicker solutions to others. Thus he must evaluate each grievance in the light of the local's over-all strategy toward management.

At least some of the local's bargaining power is reserved for pressing cases of strategic importance to the union's role in the plant. Perhaps a given supervisor has been uncooperative, and the union wishes to develop a case which will "take him down a peg or two." At other times, the local wishes to set a precedent establishing its right to be consulted in a given problem area. Thus, in one case the local vigorously protested the appointment by the company of a blood bank chairman, not because they disliked that particular man, but because they felt that since the drive was to collect blood from union men the matter should have been discussed with the local in advance.

Obtaining Optimum Support

Grievances are not bargained in a vacuum. Unless the officers receive support from the members, they find it difficult to convince management of the need and urgency of the particular issue at stake.

A former shop steward told us this story to show how his bargaining position had been seriously weakened:

> They put these oversize pieces through and they were only going to pay us the regular rate. I knew the men were worked up and behind me, so I told the company we absolutely refused to work them.
>
> First they were going to send us home; then they called me into the main office. I argued my fool head off for an hour or so and they finally said they would take them back and cut them down to size.
>
> A week after that the order came back again, only a slightly different shape, but the same oversize. I told the men they shouldn't run them, but they did. Can you imagine how I felt? I made a fool of myself arguing in front of the company and then they pulled off something like that.
>
> Well, all the superintendent had to do was walk by and smile; right then and there I decided to resign.

When a union official puts himself in the position of insisting on a particular settlement, he is relying on the men to back him up. Like a prudent poker player, he must take into account the possibility that management may well call his bluff.

Thus, management's willingness to make concessions is a function of the interest and support exhibited by the rank and file. From the union's point of view, it is important to build up member indignation, but not too far. There is always the chance that if membership feeling reaches the boiling point a grievance may set off a chain reaction, terminating in an unauthorized strike—a strike which could come at the wrong time and over the wrong issue. Even if the grievance does not lead to an immediate strike, the union may be placed in the position of having to deliver even greater benefits before the men will consider a compromise. If an immediate and favorable settlement is not forthcoming, the men may lose faith in the militancy and ability of their officers and may take matters into their own hands. In turn, in the eyes of management the union has become irresponsible, unable to discipline its own membership.

Therefore, at the outset of a grievance dispute the officers are faced with the necessity of controlling the pressure, building just the right amount.

Still more difficult, is the question of timing. Even when the parties are trying to expedite matters, negotiations over complicated issues may take months. Contract clauses setting time limits for each stage of the grievance procedure are rarely effective. In many cases, the members show "support" during the early stages of negotiations and then lapse into apathy. The officers need sustained interest on the part of the rank and file continuing over many months. It is important that the members do not dissipate their strength too early.

Maintaining Control of the Grievance Procedure

Of course, officers would like to obtain personal credit for union victories and avoid the blame for defeats. Yet, even apparent victories may backfire. Situations may change—as they did in a local which won a change in compensation for its salesmen, from commission to straight weekly salary, during a period of merchandise shortages. Shortly thereafter, the supply of goods improved and the men blamed the union for their loss of high commission earnings.

In such situations, the leaders whose names are signed to the agreement may be crucified. The lesson is simple: "Don't stick your neck out." In following this course, it becomes necessary to evaluate grievances—a complex task not for the neophyte. Even experienced officers can make serious errors in judging whether pushing a particular grievance will hurt more members than it helps (by virtue of its long-run effects on relations with management) or in judging the amount of "solidarity" or "irresponsibility" (depending on one's point of view) which the members will show on its behalf.

If the officers are to maintain their freedom to choose the cases they want to push, and thus keep their names from being identified with union defeats, they must find some way to avoid responsibility and to insulate themselves from membership pressures. One effective means of retaining control of the grievance procedure is to make it more formal. They can do this through (1) requiring members to sign grievances, (2) carefully "screening" grievances before negotiating with plant management, (3) never negotiating with management without another officer present, (4) relying on precedents and legalistic interpretations, (5) involving the International, and (6) "passing the buck" to the arbitrator.

Requiring that Members Sign

Many members feel that signing grievances puts them on the spot. They would much prefer that the formal responsibility for making a complaint against the boss be taken by a steward or higher union official.

Of course, this responsibility is just what the officers would like to avoid. They feel that by insisting upon signed grievances they can weed out the unimportant ones. Particularly when a grievance affects intergroup relations, they want the members to know that they are not taking sides. Further, if the grievance backfires, they want it clearly understood that "it wasn't our idea." On the other hand, when difficult cases arise, which the officers feel are important to win, they prefer that many of the grievances remain unwritten so that they can be handled with flexibility.

The officers feel that without a signed grievance, it is difficult to prove to the company that they have membership backing. They recall cases in which a member, having submitted a verbal grievance, backed down when management challenged his charges. Such instances give the appearance that the officers are fomenting grievances. Furthermore, some companies absolutely refuse to consider unsigned grievances.

Screening

If a steward successfully adjusts a grievance, he usually contacts an influential member of the executive board or grievance committee. Often (although the custom varies in different locals), this board member will not act further until the matter is screened by the full board.

In some locals, the screening approaches the formality of a judicial investigation, with its courtroom decorum. The aggrieved member is asked a long series of questions. Other interested parties are invited to testify. Cross-examination is allowed and when the hearing is complete, the parties are asked to leave the room and a formal vote is taken. Finally, written notices of the final decision are sent to the interested parties.

In the situations we have studied, the local officers have found such a screening committee useful. Like good lawyers, they want to know all the facts, regardless of whether these are favorable or not. If management's case is strong, the officers may wish to drop the matter and avoid embarrassment. Wherever possible, they are anxious to be prepared for the most damaging evidence the other side can present. They seek to avoid situations where they must admit:

> We just didn't have the facts. When we heard what management had to say, I asked for a recess. I told our boys that we just had to withdraw the case. Was my face red!

Furthermore, group discussion provides an excellent educational opportunity for newer grievancemen and promotes the adoption of a common policy. In this way, the screening committee also provides protection against the previously discussed proclivity of the members to "shop around." The vote of such a committee provides an ideal means of saying "no" to a demanding member when a personal refusal would be difficult. Officers who don't adopt a semblance of unity, are open to "whipsawing" by the members.

Principle of Twos

Many locals adhere to what might be called the "principle of twos." This is the unwritten rule that no union officer should ever negotiate with management *alone*. An officer who violates this is immediately suspected of "selling out." Why else should he have secret dealings with the company? The officers of such locals will tell virtuous tales like this:

> Sweeney [the superintendent] cornered me in the hallway and said he wanted to talk about the Adams case. I told him I would be glad to discuss it any time, but I had to have a steward or someone from the grievance committee with me.

Where the rule is broken, one hears rumors like this one:

> Karl went in alone on Thursday to settle the machinist apprentice grievance. Sure he got what he wanted, but he had to promise to give the company a rate concession. If he hadn't sold us out, we would have won that next grievance.

However, when there is a witness, no one can say afterwards that an officer made a private deal to the detriment of the membership.

Legalism

The discussions within the grievance committee pay considerable attention to precedents. There is little evidence of logrolling or political favoritism. Indeed, it seemed to us, as outsiders, that the officers carried their emphasis on legalism well past the point of political advantage. An example of this involved temporary summer employees in the plate shop of one local:

The plate shop was politically the most powerful group in the local; and the temporary employees were much disliked. Even the union president said of them:

"Without exception, they are sons and relatives of management. They are just a bunch of fair-haired boys on vacation from college, slumming among those who have to earn a living."

During the summer, management gave one of these temporary men an overtime assignment (naturally paying time-and-a-half). At once, the permanent members were up in arms.

As one said, "When I see some squirt going out on a Saturday, and taking away money which I can't get, then I really get mad."

The chief steward ruled that there could be no discrimination between union members. "Once a man pays his dues, he is entitled to all the rights and privileges of the contract. The contract says overtime must be divided equally among all members. They get overtime!" The executive board backed him up, fully realizing that this was politically unpopular.

Still, the emphasis on legalism does provide a useful insulation against rank-and-file pressure. By citing previous rulings or union-management agreements, they can always tell the members:

We can't reverse ourselves now. The precedent has been set already. What would the company think if we took a different position every time we met with them?

In this way, the officers can lay the blame for a politically popular decision on the rule of law.

Bringing in the International

Perhaps the most convenient means of avoiding responsibility is to master responsibility to the International's field representatives. Few locals have their own full-time business agents, but the International representative is presumably someone with experience and technical ability, an expert who can help the local officers in a tight situation.

Of course, there are disadvantages attached to bringing in an outsider: The local leaders sacrifice some of their independence and freedom of action. One International representative told us:

Many locals call us in on grievances at first. But after a while they see they are losing out by it. They see that we get the credit for it. So they avoid bringing in outside officials unless they really have to.

Involving the Arbitrator

"Passing the buck" to the arbitrator is still another way of avoiding pressure. In some instances, the local will press a weak grievance to arbitration merely because the officers feel that it is politically inexpedient to turn it down.

Sometimes this backfires. In one local, the carpenters pushed for a wage increase. The executive board was sure that there were many other groups with more worthy claims, but the carpenters occupied a politically strategic position. The case was taken to arbitration and, to the surprise of everyone, the arbitrator gave them what they asked. Naturally, other groups descended on the executive board like a wolf pack.

Conclusion

All these techniques have the effect of insulating the officers from rank-and-file pressures. They make it possible to avoid responsibility for the failure to press grievances more diligently and the unexpected effects of a grievance which has "backfired." A further objective is to minimize the number of formal cases that might clog the grievance machinery. This leaves the officers more flexibility to explore the really important problems informally.

This raises a curious paradox: On the one hand, the leadership seeks to formalize the internal aspects of the grievance procedure. On the other hand, they are anxious to make their relationship with management less formal. Formalization of these internal aspects reduces the number of union contacts with management below the top local level. As a result, there is greater concentration of the bargaining function in the hands of a small group of experts.

With this analysis of the grievance procedure, we are now ready to consider the leading figures in the life of the local—the stewards and local-wide officers—and their relationship to the rank-and-file groups with which they work.

6

The Steward: Man in the Middle

While the steward may have declined in relative importance, he still occupies an important position. When effective, he is a strategic link in the chain of communications between the rank and file and the top leadership.

The steward's position as "man in the middle" is difficult. His authority is restricted, and he is subject to almost irreconcilable pressures arising from the fact that he is a member of three different social systems—the union, the company, and the departmental work group—and, unlike the ordinary worker who may be a member of the same groups, the steward is subject to special claims for loyalty from each.

Although straddling the fence, the vast majority of stewards function in terms of one system. Depending on a primary orientation toward the work group, the union, or the company, there are three ideal types—*social leaders, active unionists,* or *self-seekers*. Of course, there are few stewards who fit any of these three categories perfectly. Still, the more extreme examples may prove further insight into the dynamics of the steward's role.

Types of Stewards

The social leader   As might be expected, many stewards are elected because they are respected and well liked by their fellow workers. The typical social leader has given up hope of promotion within the company and is not much interested in union activities. He takes the steward's job because his buddies want him to have it—and perhaps because he thinks that the title will help him to protect the men if they get in trouble.

Of course, it is impossible to fit the social leader into a single mold; more than one kind of person can win the respect of the group. Some might well be called *fixers*—men who "know the ropes" and the right people; not only are they popular within their own work group, but they have important contacts in both union and management. They make subtle use of such "pressures" as implied threats of slowdowns, promises to deliver the department vote at the next union election, and the menace of demonstrations at meetings. All these are effective in winning high priority for the department's grievances. They prefer to do things quietly and on the basis of personal contact, and firmly eschew formal grievances. Jack Stero provides an example of this type. He was obviously an important man in the shop. He had connections outside the plant too, particularly with local gamblers. The men considered him shrewd and cautious, with lots of native intelligence.

The *social worker* approaches life differently. Usually he is an older man who takes a patriarchal point of view toward his constituents. To give him a grievance is not a matter of principle, but a family rift which should be healed quickly. One such steward described his approach to grievances:

> I first try to find out what is wrong. It usually isn't the job; it is something they've done the night before or some trouble they are in outside. You see, I know all the people here. I'm needed because many people get too excited when they go into the main office; they tend to forget who they are talking to. We don't get as much for them as they want every time . . . but we usually manage to work out something with the boss.

The active unionist   In contrast to the social leaders the active unionists, are the men who accept stewardship because they believe in the union and want power and prestige. Often they aspire to eventual election to local-wide office. They attend meetings religiously and form the backbone of the minor union committees. Active unionists vary considerably in how they get along with their fellow workers. Some have many friends, others are merely respected for their abilities in handling grievances. In a few cases it seemed that the individual in question became active as a form of compensation for his lack of popularity.

Active unionists approach their job from several points of view. Some are

primarily interested in promotion within the union and do everything possible
to win the attention of the officers and the rank and file as a whole. They
speak vigorously at meetings and give the impression of acting courageously.
One *steward-politician* gave his formula for getting ahead:

> The important thing is to make an issue. Perhaps some company policy
> has been hurting people and nothing has been done about it. Speak the way
> you think people are feeling. Be careful not to attack any individual, he may
> fight back.
>
> Griping about poor working conditions and giving the impression that if
> you had the chance, you would do something about it, always helps.

Others are concerned with building the union as an institution. One such
organizer, who had a short but active career, recounted:

> Every so often you'd hear a couple of guys really lambasting the foreman
> in the washroom—that's where you can really hear the gripes. But when I'd
> write up the grievance and take it to the fellows, they'd say it was too small.
> I'd say "the hell with you" and push it anyway.
>
> Soon the company would be coming to me and saying, "Those guys don't
> have a grievance. They're perfectly satisfied." And I'd say, "The hell they
> don't. If you don't want to recognize it, I'll take it to the next step." I didn't
> care if the guys supported me, I went through with it.

Or take the case of Sam Levino as described by one of the men in his
department:

> One of the guys just bought a bottle of milk and was sort of complaining
> out loud that the damn milk was sour. Sam heard, came running over,
> grabbed the bottle of milk, took it back to the cafeteria and demanded they
> give him a new bottle. The man whose milk it was said: "Who does he think
> he is? If I wanted to complain, I could have brought it back myself."

Some are so overbearing, so anxious to press grievances, that the top officers
fear they will hurt the union. Bob Rockstow, for example, was not well liked
by other men in his department because he was high-strung and officious.
He rarely missed membership meetings, and often antagonized the officers.
One of them, talking about an unnecessary grievance which he had filed
said:

> The trouble is that there are too many stewards with rough edges. They
> like to throw their weight around and as a result, management gets tired. It
> isn't necessary to push every point.

The executive board decided not to have him fill a temporary vacancy as
chief steward on the grounds that he wasn't tactful.

Other stewards, particularly in craft unions, took a more passive view of

their jobs. They were *policemen*—if the company violated the economic provisions of the contract, they would go into action. But in general they pre-
ferred to keep the peace, and rarely were interested in "petty" membership
complaints, such as how the foreman treated individuals.

Self-seekers   Some stewards are accused of accepting the job just for
what "they can get out of it." In some cases, this charge seems to be true:
their chief motive in accepting the union office is that of individual economic
self-interest. Either they want to adjust personal grievances of their own or
they want to bring themselves to the attention of management for possible
promotion.

In either case, the self-seeker thinks primarily in terms of his own job and
advancement, and is especially sensitive to his relations with the company.
As will be seen, such an individual is not likely to be elected, except in departments which have serious internal weaknesses or a high degree of de-
moralization regarding union activity.

One steward told us frankly:

> I know the guys in my department hate me and would get me if they
> could. But I got the business in that grievance two years ago and I'm not
> going to quit until I revenge that licking no matter what happens.

Of a female steward it was said:

> She's a spitfire. She really fights. But the main reason that she got in was
> a selfish grievance of her own [relating to a pay increase].

Dan Nelson was a steward for a number of older men, most of whom were
near retirement age, and none of whom was active in the union. Prior to the
war he had been a first-class machinist. When he came back from service,
the company gave him second-class duties although continuing his first-class
pay. His only topic of conversation, and sole purpose in life, was to regain
his old line of work.

Some stewards accept the job as a first step toward promotion into management.

> Stewardship for him is an avenue for meeting and conferring with man-
> agement officials. If astute enough he can impress both management and
> workers with his ability. . . . So concerned is he with convincing manage-
> ment of his ability that he presents workers' grievances with special zeal.
> He hopes to impress management with the idea that he could do an equally
> good job if he were a foreman and had to fight grievances.[1]

[1] Delbert C. Miller and William H. Form, *Industrial Sociology* (New York: Harper &
Row, 1951), 265–66.

Relationship of Steward to Department Attitudes

Under what circumstances are these three types of individuals elected stewards? How do they behave in office? The answer to these questions seems to have a great deal to do with the relationship between departmental work groups and the two other social systems with which the steward is in contact—the union and the company.

For example, some departments typically have a number of outstanding problems, but lack the political strength to force the officers to give priority to their demands. Often they are involved in a dispute with another department over an issue such as seniority. Yet, even when the real enemy is the company, they realize that to win their grievance battles they need union support.

A steward in such a department may find his job "rough going." On the one hand, as a steward he is subject to pressures from the top officers to conform to union policy. On the other hand, the members of his small group want him to put their interests first. This dilemma is intensified if he feels that in bucking the local-wide leadership on small issues he will lose their support on larger ones. A local vice-president pointed out the conflict which can arise under these circumstances:

> The other men in the department really put pressure on you. They want you to do something which is contrary to the interests of the local.
>
> In a case like that, it is up to the real union leader to try to educate the people around him so they will become aware of the fact that what hurts the union, hurts them. This is pretty rough going at times. Sometimes it may not even be true.
>
> In that case, he should be honest and admit it. He should place the choice pretty clearly up to the people with him so they can realize what the issues are and decide by themselves.

A case example may illustrate this conflict:

> Both the burners and the welders felt they should be eligible for a newly posted high-paying job. After hearing evidence from both sides, the union executive board ruled in favor of the welders. However, the company wanted the burners to have the job, and the union was loath to go to arbitration. As a means of frustrating the company's desires, the executive board instructed the steward in the burner department to advise his men not to bid for the job.

Several of the senior burners, who had applied before the steward could contact them, agreed with great reluctance to withdraw their bid. However, just before the deadline, an apprentice burner (a young man in the department) made his application and got the job! The other burners felt they had been double-crossed and started harassing the steward. As he put it:

I think I have lost all my friends. Last night my phone rang at three in the morning. Bill Mulligan was a little stewed and he cussed me out for five minutes till I hung up on him. Even the wives call up my wife. I hate to go to work in the morning.

Within a week he resigned his office. The new steward was considerably less enthusiastic about implementing union policy.

The following is an example of a common political process—that in which a representative can get action from higher authorities only insofar as he is willing to do favors for them in return. Ed Waloughski was successful in this. Although he frequently missed union meetings and had refused an important union position which was offered to him, his contacts with the local president and the International representative were excellent. When issues arose which concerned his own department, he exerted great power behind the scenes. There was an implicit agreement between Waloughski and the top local officers. He supplied them with political support, while they gave high priority to the grievances which arose in his department.

In the case just cited, the position of the steward was made easier by the fact that his department had problems which could be settled. The exchange of favors was easy to make. If either the officers or the work group ask too much, then the steward's position becomes difficult, if not untenable. In such circumstances, the social leader often resigns. One such told us:

Some people never forget. They figure once you did something wrong by them, they will always hold it in for you. I wanted to be friends with everybody, so I gave it up.

If the union is strong, someone presumably in the good graces of the top union officers will be elected. However, if the union is weak, it may appear better strategy to elect someone who can get along with management. One department, which was dissatisfied with working conditions and completely distrustful of the top local officers, constantly elected straw bosses as stewards. It was felt that management would be more likely to listen to these men, who were in part responsible for production, than to someone more militant. An adjacent department elected the foreman's brother-in-law. However, when the weak leadership was defeated and the union took on a more militant tone, there was a complete change-over among the stewards.

Dependent departments face a recurring dilemma every time elections roll around. Active unionists and self-seekers might have good relations with union and management, but are not always anxious to support the group's particular grievance. Social leaders, on the other hand, are sometimes *persona non grata* outside their own department.

One large department, which was studied intensively, was never able to solve this problem. Stewards were changed as regularly as clockwork. For many years this department had been faced with an almost insoluble problem. The men normally worked fifteen to twenty hours of overtime per week and were demanding a major cut in this heavy schedule without a reduction in take-home pay! Steward after steward tried to work out some acceptable plan, but each time negotiations began, rumors would circulate that the men were going to have to take a cut in take-home pay. Some stewards resigned, some became discouraged, and others accepted the attitude of the top officers—that the department was trying to get something for nothing. A long-service employee in the department described the various stewards that had come and gone:

> Bob Wilson was a good effective leader, but then he got tired. You can't battle those boys [the top local officers] too long and he quit.
>
> Gus Monohan was a personable guy. Everyone liked him, but this union business was beyond his comprehension. He just didn't think it was possible for us to get anything through the union.
>
> John Marson was a scrapper. Then after he came home wounded from the war, he gave up. I think the boys got management to make a pitch to him. Anyway he ended up as an inspector [a promotion].
>
> If you did not cooperate with them, they [the officers] would pigeonhole your grievances and then start putting pressure on you to get things done. You had to have the entire gang behind you if you were going to stand up against stuff like that, and I guess the members didn't realize what was happening.
>
> If you still weren't a good boy, there was another way to bribe you. There were committees and they [officers] put you on them—$5.00 a night, even if you didn't show up. Three committees meant $15.00.

The groups we have been describing believe they can achieve their objectives *through* the union. Hostile groups are those that have given up hope. They are actively opposed to the incumbent leadership and rely primarily on self-help techniques. Here the active unionist has little chance of election. The group will often select its most competent social leader to represent its interests with management and to "protect" itself against the union.

Other such departments don't even bother to fill the steward's office—or when they do, they show their contempt through electing an inebriate, a clown, an ambitious pain-in-the-neck, or a very low-status worker.

For example, in one local a department which was openly advocating a rival union elected as steward a crotchety old worker who had been placed on a semiactive job. The members took the attitude: "We didn't think he would get anything done, but he sure got in the foreman's hair."

Of course, in some cases in their anxiety to oppose the union they elect a self-seeker who takes the uncontested office to further his own interests. When his motives become sufficiently clear, he is often repudiated in favor of a social leader.

In some apathetic departments, no one is willing to make the race. However, if the union places enough pressure on the group, they may elect someone. At times, social leaders will take the job as a form of "noblesse oblige." A business agent told us:

> Bill Allison is the steward of the sheetlayers. It is a shame they have a man like that. He doesn't believe in the union at all. He would rather go out and get drunk with the boys. But to tell you the truth, there isn't anybody in the department who believes in the union. He was a nice fellow who everybody liked. We told them they had to elect somebody or we wouldn't touch their grievances. So they elected him. And we are stuck with it.

Conclusion

It would be misleading to give the impression that all stewards can be easily classified under one of the three categories: social leader, active unionist, and self-seeker. Many stewards assiduously push grievances, attend meetings, and take part in other union activities and still are respected and looked to for guidance by their fellow workers.

Yet, all stewards do not perceive their jobs in the same light. In part, this is a product of distinctive personalities and past experience. Some stewards seek authority and prestige, others popularity within the group or even promotion to management. Some look for grievances, others try to minimize them.

To a large degree however, the stewards' behavior is shaped by problems which they all must face. In one sense, the steward serves as a communications link to management and higher union officials. On the other hand, he is expected to gain departmental conformity to policies laid down by the top officers. Thus, his success as a steward depends both upon the type of relationship he can develop his ability to integrate the leadership's demands with the expectations of the men he represents.

The steward's task is relatively easy if the work group is united and has proved its political influence (as in "pro-union" groups), or if the interests of union and work groups are more or less identical (as in groups which are "moderately pro-union").

Stewards in departments with other viewpoints find that reconciliation of their several roles is more difficult. Where the problems are not too serious, or the steward possesses great personal ability, such reconciliation is possible. Otherwise, retention of the office can endanger his popularity within his own work group.

Under these circumstances, social leaders may either resign or seek to obtain the group's objectives through self-help techniques. Active unionists will support the union even against the interests of their own group.

7

The Local-wide Leader

The discussion so far has dealt with the workers' departmental representatives, their stewards. In this chapter, we shall deal with the small group of active leaders who did the bulk of the local's work. Most of these were top union officers, although some were part of what might be called the "active opposition," and a few were even stewards. These were the men who carried most of the responsibility, these were the work horses who maintained the union's day-to-day function. Without them, the paid business agents and International representatives would be swamped with work and, in many cases completely out of touch with the rank and file.

In undertaking this study, we have attempted to find answers to these questions: What are the basic personality characteristics of the leader? How does his union activity affect his job? What kinds of satisfaction does he derive from union leadership? What is his relationship to his family and his community? And finally, on a more hypothetical level, is there any relationship between the leader's behavior and his aspiration "to get ahead in the world"?

Naturally, the leaders observed cannot be described by a single complex of character traits—nor did their behavior appear uniform. However, enough common traits showed themselves repeatedly in interviews and observations to make generalizations meaningful.

Personality Characteristics

Union leaders appear to be men whose energies and creative urges are insufficiently challenged by their everyday life. They seem to find in union activity a means of expression which is missing elsewhere. They have apparently inexhaustible vigor and are dissatisfied with the world around them.

High activity level   One of the chief elements which distinguish union leaders as a class is their high activity level. They have a tremendous urge to do things. They never seem to tire. Again and again one hears comments such as: "I'm like iron—the harder you hit me, the stronger I am." "I can't help it; I just like to work."

Being an officer is an exhausting job. Local meetings sometimes last four or five hours, while negotiations often last the entire day and into the night—but most officers seem to thrive on it. In one local, the officers had to attend seven regularly scheduled meetings monthly. Another local negotiated four or five days a week for nine consecutive months before reaching an agreement with the company.

Key officers spend even more time on the regular day-to-day routine of the union. One gave this explanation of why he was tired:

> I was over at the office from noon on yesterday. There was an executive board meeting after supper. That lasted until I had to go back to work at midnight. I got two hours sleep after coming back from work, but I had to go back to the office, and it looks like I won't get more than three hours sleep before I get back to work again, in the plant.

Thus, this man had but five hours' sleep in forty-eight hours. Other leaders exhibit equal stamina. One regularly spends six or seven hours in the plant on his own time handling grievances. From there he goes to the union office to write letters and often has to attend a local meeting the same night. He is both grievance chairman and recording secretary for his local. This involves him with almost every grievance case and all the correspondence of the local.

One local president kept a careful diary. This showed that over a year's period he attended 240 meetings (in addition to grievance conferences with management) and contributed a total of 1,500 uncompensated hours to his local.

Many officials are equally active in nonunion organizations. Here is a representative comment:

> My wife is really getting mad at me. There is this executive board meeting tonight and membership meeting tomorrow and a shop meeting on Wednesday. Thursday, there is an installation in a fraternal organization I belong to. Friday, there is a rehearsal for the show the men's club at the church is

putting on. After that, the Knights—I'll have to push to make both. Saturday, we're going out; on Sunday we put on our show.

All this activity, it should be emphasized, is in addition to the regular jobs these local officers hold. Even when they draw some income from the union—in the form of allowances for such things as gasoline, lunches, and stationery, or reimbursement for actual lost time—those with heavy family responsibilities must supplement it in other ways. Some are skilled craftsmen and do carpentry, painting, and so on. Others, particularly in small cities, work their own farms, drive taxis, sell real estate, and so on.

Nervous tension   With the surplus of nervous energy that these men apparently have, it is not surprising that many are afflicted with psychosomatic illnesses. Many officials claim present or past symptoms of ulcers and similar conditions having a potential emotional basis.

In part, these conditions may be the result of spending too much time on union affairs. The evidence suggests, however, that many of these illnesses would have developed even if the men concerned had never joined the union. Indeed, union activity may even have improved their condition.

One leader, who had suffered a mental breakdown just before he was elected steward, said, "That job pulled me right out of it; it gave me something to do." At the time, he was already working sixty to seventy hours a week on his job, serving on the State Guard, and bringing up two children. Then, later, having not been reelected, he said of his union activity:

> I used to put three or four nights a week into it. I miss it terribly. You won't believe it, but I'm taking phenobarbital. I can't sleep nights. When I see the kinds of decisions that are being made, it just burns me up.

Another man, who had been relatively inactive for some time and who was working on a job he could never leave during his shift to talk to others, developed a serious ulcer attack the afternoon he was to meet the International president. A third, became seriously ill shortly after being defeated for major office. As soon as he got well he became active again. He remarked, "This kind of stuff gets into your blood. You don't want to quit, but it gets you tired and tense."

An officer who came near to resigning his office permanently, had this to say about his close call:

> You know I was set to resign yesterday. I figured my life would then be so much easier: walk into the plant and not worry about anyone jumping you on a case.
>
> Well, it felt so good to think that way for a while. Then I took the resignation back, and I'm glad that I did it now. I guess I couldn't live without this union business. You get so used to it. I don't know what it is; maybe it's the challenge of some of the cases you have to handle.

It's a rotten business though in a way. I hate this walking into a bar and having some guy jump you and call you names, and not be able to do anything about it. They just don't seem to have any respect for union officials, but I just couldn't give it up.

Idealism and discontent   Being an active union leader requires the expenditure of so much time and energy that selfish economic motivation is not enough. Self-seekers are less often found on this level. With few exceptions, union leaders are idealistic. They are anxious to change things and build a better world. They see the union as the best means they have to achieve this end. One of them said:

> I wanted to do something where I actually would be trying to make the world a better place, and the labor movement is about the only place where I can do that.

Union leaders, as a rule, are dissatisfied with the world as it exists today. They feel that their lives offer insufficient opportunity for themselves and "their kind." In the words of one leader:

> Unionism is something born in you; you have got to believe in it; it is something deep down in your heart. You have to have a feeling of revolt, and mind you, I'm not a radical. It's not only that; it is psychology. It's a feeling of aggression. It's a drive. It's wanting to be on the move; it's being noisy. It's the kind of man who'll get ahead anywhere.

Their lives and their jobs in the plant are not very satisfactory. One leader said poignantly:

> Today I wrote a letter to my congressman. He's supposed to be in Washington for me, to vote for me, and I don't like the way he's doing it. That makes me sound pretty important, doesn't it?
>
> Do you think I am that important? Well, I'm not, not as important as a stalk of celery. I'm just a rotten little cog in a big industrial wheel. You know why? Well, I'll tell you, because I work like a horse and don't accomplish a damn thing. I make a living by fighting with management for every dime, and that is all.
>
> Satisfaction in my work? Why, hell, anyone can do my work in the shop. What kind of satisfaction can you get from a job like that? But the real trouble is my efforts aren't appreciated. Oh sure, my family knows I work hard and they're grateful, but I don't mean that kind of appreciation. I mean that to the world as a whole I mean nothing, and I'm so damn typical it makes me sick.

They are critical of the company. They feel that, somehow, they haven't gotten an "even break." As one said:

> One of the worst things the company does during negotiations is to bring in these new young fellows that they're trying to show the ropes to. They say,

"This is Joe Doaks from M.I.T. and Frank Jones from Cornell and he studied so many years here, and this guy studied so many years there," and well, the fellows get a little upset at that. I know one year Hanson, the president of the local, told them, after they got done that he was Sloppy Joe from Nowhere and he was in a hurry to get back. I know this sort of thing makes most of the fellows feel as if they wished they had a lot more education and a college degree behind them when they go in to bargain with the company.

Union leaders are also critical of their fellow officers and dissatisfied with their own union jobs. Some of their descriptions of union office would make the unwary investigator wonder why they ever accepted such a position. For example:

You've got to remember that to be a union officer, you take an awful lot of trouble on your shoulders—trouble everywhere and a thankless job to boot. You fight with your wife for going out too many nights. You fight with the international representatives, you fight with the men, you fight with the company, you're always fighting. If you spend too much time up at the front office settling grievances up there, the men get into fights back in the plant, and you should be back there settling those.

Officers complain that they have to hear everybody's problems, show an interest in them, and attempt to provide some solution. In doing so they place themselves in the middle of petty disagreements among the men, and involve themselves in burdensome expenditures of time and energy. They feel they receive little compensation for all this service—certainly as compared to that received by management officials with comparable responsibilities. The time and duties involved endanger their relationships, not only with their fellow workers but also with the company and their families. The fact remains that they must provide real satisfactions, for there is intense competition for many high union jobs.

The wives are often critical of their husbands' outside preoccupations. They resent the restrictions on their own social family life that result. The wife of a chairman of a grievance committee bitterly exclaimed:

There is no question about how I feel about these union meetings. I begrudge any time at all that Bill puts into these activities. Don't misunderstand; I'm in favor of the union all right, but the guy is never home, or else he is sleeping, and he doesn't sleep much at that. Why, do you know that this week the secretary at the union office called just to tell me that my husband was almost at the breaking point. Imagine! People actually calling to tell me about my own husband. I was so embarrassed.

Many of the wives have brought pressure on their husbands to give up their union activity. They object to the time it takes, not to the fact that it is *union* activity, for in many cases they apparently have considerable interest in their husbands' activities.

Relationship to Job

A common stereotype among those who have relatively little experience with union leaders is that they are recruited from the "worst" elements in the factory. While this may be true in some situations, our study found little evidence of it.

A substantial minority of the top local officials we observed were at one time opposed to unions. As one officer commented:

> When I first met Malony and DiBruzzo [the organizers] I thought one looked like a crook and the other like a typical New York sharpie. That's what I expected union people to look like.

Most of the men, when first hired, devoted the same energy to their jobs that they now give to the union. As one official thought back:

> When I got my first job, I was over at Chestnut Street. The men over there were goofing off. I started to put in what I thought was a day's work. The other men told me to take it easy. One of them said, "You can't be promoted. I've been here twelve years and this is as far as I've gotten." I said, "If this is as far as you've gotten and you've been here twelve years, I'm not taking your advice." I guess I scabbed the rates.

Indeed, many have been in the lower ranks of management. The president of a local lost his foreman's job during a cutback in the ranks of supervision. The most aggressively anti-management officer of another local had once been a foreman. He continued to fight for the proposition that union members who are promoted to foreman should retain their seniority rights as workers.

The vice-president of a clerical local became active in the union only after he failed to obtain a promotion despite his excessive management orientation:

> I'd been pushing the production workers too hard on this new incentive plan. I believed the system could work, and would work if it was pushed hard enough. We could make people like it. Top management didn't support us and I guess I stuck my neck out too far once. Well, anyhow, the other guy got the job and I was plenty sore for a time even though I knew he was a capable man and probably deserved it.
>
> I decided that if management was going to play that way, I could play just as hard against them as I was willing to play with them. . . . I worked as hard as I knew how, but now I'm going to do just the opposite. I'm going to work hard for the union.

Even those who are not actually in supervisory positions have attained a high level of job competency. Many union officers are on the top of their promotional ladders—as will be discussed in the next chapter.

Even when officers speak favorably about the company, many still express fears regarding management's "real" opinions of their union activity. As active union officers they have certain safeguards and protections that would be absent should they again assume a position in the rank and file. One local president observed:

> Sometimes you think of dropping out of the union, and then you think it might be a pretty dangerous thing. You don't want to be out there where the company can get you. You know, recently I've done some things and spoken of the company in terms that maybe they'd like to get me too. I know they are after another officer, and I can't forget how they got rid of old Burnello.

Another president said:

> If you're no longer an officer, that means that the company can get something on you more easily too. Of course, I've got a pretty good record. Since I took office, there have been no walkouts. Oh, we've had wildcats for a little while in some departments, but there have been no strikes, and that is really a feather in my cap.

Most union leaders go right ahead with their work in the union in spite of the fact that union activity is dangerous or believed so. Some stewards will let their doubts as to job security affect their activities. These men never become *active* leaders. Active leaders recognize (and even glory in) the risks they take.

Yet, fear of loss of job may well be in a declining phase; as management becomes more sophisticated, it learns that retaliation does not pay off. Many leaders believe that management is friendly to them as individuals:

> Management knows we're not attacking them personally, that we're just doing our job. When they've done something wrong, we tell them; and when they're right, we're willing to admit that too.

A large number of leaders were convinced that management did not hold them responsible for the outbursts of the membership or of the more radical leaders.

Here and there a different problem has come up. Management has begun the practice of hiring supervisory employees out of the active union ranks. It recognizes that the union is an effective instrument in detecting potential supervisory ability among the rank and file. Over a period of ten years, in one local, the secretary and about a third of the executive committee took jobs outside the bargaining unit. As a consequence, the union became known by its opponents as the "high road to management."

In another situation, about 25 per cent of the foremen came from the ranks of the union, and the assistant to the personnel director is a former union officer. It is an increasingly common practice to hire formal local officials as personnel directors.

Other union leaders tell how their own positions with the rank and file have been made difficult by some previous official's acceptance of a management job. In their words, "Now they think we're *all* ready to sell out."

Certainly many leaders who might have accepted promotions into management before they became active in the union feel that social pressure and the union's code of ethics prevent them from "selling out" after they become active. Where the union has a good relationship with management, however, such changes in allegiance may be easier to make. Even in situations where there is bitterness between the union and the company, union officials often accept promotions into semisupervisory positions (jobs within the bargaining unit that can still involve some management functions). In so doing, they merely postpone the inevitable decision—whether or not to cast their lot with the company and leave the union entirely.

Where union officials have "made the break," the results are often unsatisfactory. Many of the former management men say that they find greater happiness and freedom as union officials:

> The union made a man out of me. I used to be a foreman before the union came in. I had to skin the men alive; I had to be mean. I had to run after them. I had to keep them popping. I hated the job and the men hated me, and I don't blame them. I would never take the job again.

Another said:

> I've had a chance to sit on the other side of the fence, too. And let me tell you, it's no pleasure. When management has a conference, they ask if there are any questions but they really don't want any answers. You have to shut up; you can't say what you feel. You never speak your mind. Now it's just the opposite in the union. I feel always that I can say what I want to.

On the other hand, the most rabid anticompany officials often say confidentially that they think they could have done a good job in management. A union president who was fired for fomenting an excessive series of wildcat strikes confided:

> One thing, I always sort of wished I could have gone into personnel work. I know who to kick in the pants and who to pat on the shoulder, using psychology. I think I would have done it pretty well.
>
> The company could learn a lot from some of us. Not only that, we don't think the men are always right; they're not. There are plenty of fellows who are out just looking for trouble, who've laid down on the job and don't have legitimate complaints.

Another top union official compared his abilities in dealing with men with those of the personnel directors with whom he bargained. He concluded:

> I could do a hell of a lot better job than those guys. They don't know how to work with people. They figure they've got to maintain their distance from a fellow, keep talking down to him, but they don't know how much you can

get out of a guy by making out that you're at his level. If I could only take that personnel job, I'd show those guys.

Although in a few instances union activity may be a "sour grapes" substitute for promotion, our evidence suggests that a large proportion of union leaders aspire to much more than top-paying jobs and foremanships. Often, the leaders evidence conscious or unconscious desires to move entirely out of the working class. A former local president, who is now International representative, was successful for a time in starting his own chemical manufacturing plant. Others, as we have said, have been salesmen and real estate men. A few seem to reject the traditional American goals of economic success altogether and seek achievement in terms of power, respect, and authority.

Satisfactions from Leadership

Despite the headaches, however, the fact remains that union leaders do obtain real, basic satisfactions from their union work which they find nowhere else in life. To a greater or lesser extent, union activity gives them (1) a sense of achievement and constructive accomplishment, (2) an outlet for aggressions, (3) an intellectual outlet—an opportunity to use their intelligence, (4) relief from the endless monotony of many industrial jobs, (5) opportunities to increase their prestige in the eyes of management and the rank and file, and finally (6) a social outlet.

Achievement   The union leader finds in his activity a challenge, a chance to be creative, which he misses on his job. Three months after he was elected one officer said:

> We're building quite a union. I never thought it would be this interesting, but it's fascinating. Why, just to watch the local president argue grievances is educational. That's quite a sight.

Handling grievances, negotiating a contract, marshaling political support, making a speech—all these are skills of a high order. Good leaders are proud of their ability to deal with complex problems involving the different social and ethnic groups in their plants. One able local president told us this:

> I like the opportunity this job gives me to meet people, to see the different types in management and even among the workforce. In fact, when I used to work at the aircraft plant, I enjoyed sitting in the train station when I was commuting and talking to different people. I got so I could pick out what a man's work was and where he worked. Although this job of grievance-man takes an awful lot of time, if you ask me, it requires a lot more intelligence than most supervisors have. There is a lot to this business. You have to know an awful lot about the jobs and the contract, and be watching your step all the time.

These leaders object to neophytes who mishandle their work. As one put it:

> We do things much better than the other local does. Our stewards are trained. They know what to do. Those men just don't spend the time on it.

A successful leader gets great satisfaction from dealing with people. He enjoys the complexities of union politics and gets a special thrill when he is able to "put one over" on management. One leader told us:

> I was a bartender for a while, and believe me, I learned a lot about people there, and ever since then I've taken a lot of pride in being able to figure people out—how they respond to things.
> Now take Palermo. When I go in to see him, I pound on the table, shout and yell, do everything but stand on my head. That impresses him, and finally he says, "You know, Tom, when I deal with you, I always give in," and he does. With Harris you can go in there and lay all your cards on the table, and then he is going to do the same. If he figures you're right, he'll give in right away. If not, you have some arguing on your hands to accomplish anything but with him it is all straightforward.

Much of the discussion between leaders before and after meetings is devoted to exchanging stories about successful dealings with the company or with the rank and file. Bill Jones tells how he has the maintenance supervisor eating out of his hand. Bob Smith tells how he handled the troublemaker over in Building 21. Mike Stranahan brags about how he persuaded the joint union-management committee that his incentive system was best.

As a rule, a good union officer knows just about everything that there is to know about his union. Even in locals with over a thousand members, many leaders know where each member works, the nature of his job, and the "guy's personality." We were continually surprised during the executive committee meetings at the extent to which members knew the detailed background of every grievance. One leader, when complimented upon his knowledge, said, "You have to know all these things. After all, people are our stock in trade."

Many leaders carry this policy much further than is necessary. Some memorize seniority lists, just as a baseball fan memorizes the batting averages. In each case, it is from sheer love of the game.

Means for expressing aggressions   In addition, union activity is a socially approved outlet for aggression. We found that the average leader is bored with his work in the plant and frequently frustrated by a situation in which he feels management gets all the better things in life while making everything as hard as possible for the workers. To him, the union provides an opportunity to "blow off steam." During negotiations, a union leader may safely insult his boss in a manner which would be slanderous in any other context. It is small wonder that the union movement has, at times, attracted men who are almost psychopathically aggressive.

Intellectual outlet The aggressive function of union leadership can easily be exaggerated. The most violent of the leaders are often not re-elected after the organizing period is over. Most of the others get far less satisfaction from blowing up at management than from presenting a well-organized rational argument. Like a good lawyer, the union leader takes pleasure in a workman-like job of advocacy and is very upset when he does not do so good a job as he thinks he should:

> I really looked silly. The supervisor asked me questions I just didn't know how to answer. That shows you how important *preparation* is—regardless of how small the matter may be.

Union activity is thus an intellectual outlet. It gives the leaders a chance to use their imaginations and intelligence in a manner never required by their plant jobs. Union leadership offers workers a chance to fulfill the perfectly normal human desire to be a "big shot," to be independent. It offers somewhat the very same satisfaction and excitement that a small entrepreneur enjoys.

A substantial proportion of leaders become so interested in the union that they spend their spare time reading about unionism and industrial relations in spite of their many other activities. One leader told us he always read before he went to bed, chiefly about labor and economics. Another called this type of activity his form of relaxation. A third said:

> I gripe about the other faction. They hate to study facts. How can they learn their jobs unless they study? Why, I even studied back to the Bible. They had strikes even then, although they didn't call themselves unions.

Another leader mentioned that he had Philip Taft's textbook by his bedside. He, too, was impressed with the long history of unions. A local president gave the place of honor on his parlor table to seven or eight books dealing with his International and unionism in general. A local treasurer asked us to get him a book on union accounting, and one officer earned himself the name of "Mr. Prentice-Hall" for his erudition.

Relief from monotony Another element should be considered: although union meetings are normally held after the quitting whistle blows, a leader derives certain additional satisfactions while on the job.

First of all, there is time out from work—so-called "lost time." The opportunity to "check out" and handle a grievance provides a welcome break from a day's monotony, even if this break is only for a few minutes. For example, one official said:

> Union office gives you a chance to think. It keeps you active. I couldn't take it going to the plant and working at my job eight hours a day, and day in and day out doing the same things. This way you get on some very interesting things. I wish I had more training though, but I guess I'll never really get a chance to get back to school.

Grievance handling is infinitely more interesting than assembly-line work, and one can easily understand why many leaders are more than pleased when an easy grievance comes up to divert their attention. Also, when leaders are supposedly working they can make their jobs more interesting by engaging in union business—passing the word around about important union decisions, collecting dues, selling tickets. One leader told us he always looked forward to a particular tour of duty which permitted him to move all over the plant, saying frankly, "When I'm on that trick I never get much work done. I spend my time—at least half of it—talking union."

Thus, the union provides important satisfactions through relieving the ordinary humdrum existence of the plant.

Economic rewards   Few leaders seek full-time jobs as business agents or International representatives. Only two ever mentioned the possibility of going on the International payroll, although with probing a number admitted that they had thought about it.

One man, who at the time had an excellent chance of being appointed organizer, said:

> I would like to try it for a while to see if I like it. It would mean putting out a lot more work and neglecting my family even more than I have, but the possibility is very interesting.

Another was less certain:

> I used to think that I could get a job with the international office, but I would never make good. I would get too excited. I would be much better at administrative work. Of course, I would like to try some. Don't say I want it, though if I had a chance I would take it.

For the most part the union leaders studied felt that their chances of getting on the full-time payroll were so slim that few had well-considered thoughts as to whether they would accept. In any case, the pay of the average organizer or business agent is so little higher than the usual salary that is paid to the skilled worker, that the financial attractions of the job are rather slight.

Even part-time leaders, of course, receive some compensation. Wages lost during working hours are reimbursed by "lost-time payments." For the time spent outside working hours, "supper money" or the equivalent is paid, although the practice varies from local to local. One local allows $3 a night, plus actual auto-parking charges. Another pays its official a flat $25 a month (called "salary" by the treasurer). A third gives its recording and financial secretaries $30 a month. It is also common practice to pay members of a committee (such as the recreation committee) for the nights they work.

One of the highly desired compensations for union activity, is the chance to go to state and national union conventions, company-wide bargaining meetings, and the like. The delegates enjoy all-expense-paid trips to great metropolitan centers that they might otherwise never have visited.

Of the locals we studied, payments to officers comprised 30 to 60 per cent of total union costs (other than the per capita tax paid to the International). This may sound like a lot, but taking into account the extra transportation, entertainment, and meal costs incurred by the leaders, in almost every case their out-of-pocket costs exceed what they receive from the unions.

In total, then, financial motives for union activities are not great. Perhaps more important than any immediate money advantage, is the fact that many unions offer their leaders almost complete job security in the form of super-seniority. One man spoke about seniority this way:

> You know, I've had a lot of trouble with my wife because of all this union work—she doesn't seem to understand. But I continue, because I feel I've done a lot for my family to make their position more secure.

Prestige   Although the financial advantages are limited, union leadership does provide an opportunity to gain higher status or prestige in the eyes of one's fellow workers and of management. A former union officer commented:

> You bet I was pretty proud of having jumped from a steward over eighteen men to secretary of the whole organization.

After a departmental meeting, another confided:

> Did you notice how they kept looking to me for leads on all the things that were brought up? Even though I'm not grievanceman over there any more, they still look to me for these things.

An executive board member who had not chosen to run said this about the incentives for taking office:

> Well, it's just like why does a man ever want to be President of the United States. That is a damn fool thing to do. There is much more work connected with it than anything else, but an awful lot of people want it. It is for the prestige involved.
>
> The same holds for union office. You're a big shot. Well, not really a big shot but an important fellow among the guys in the shop. Now take Hal (the union president), for example. I think he is a lot more sure of himself since he became president than he ever was before. He has grown in office too. He

is really an important man in the plant as a union officer. People have to come to you with things, and you make decisions.

Union activity increases the worker's prestige in the eyes of management, and he glories in it. The leaders expect to sit down with management as equals, and are extremely sensitive to slurs upon their position. They make a point of this in contract negotiations and grievance bargaining. Here is an example of the kind of story leaders like to tell of how they treated management:

> Right in the middle of something Phil [the chief union negotiator] was saying, Ransom [the company negotiator] got up and without saying anything left the room. So as soon as he came back and started talking, Phil got up too and walked out. You have got to teach them to give us respect. We represent the men and are just as important as they.

Here is another example:

> The division head picked up his paper while I was talking to him, so I picked up mine as soon as he started talking. There we were, like a bunch of kids. When will the company grow up and treat us like men?

A local president told of his conversation with a department head:

> Alton told me he wanted to talk to me, so I said, "Okay, Mr. Alton, what's on your mind?"
> He said, "That so-and-so McNulty [the chief steward] is really getting on my nerves. I wish to hell you'd get him off me." So I told him, "Mr. Alton, Mr. McNulty is the chief steward of this department. As such, he is on the same level as you are. You are in charge of management for this department, and he is in charge of the union. I want you to treat him in the same way you expect him to treat you. I'm telling you this, Mr. Alton, as president of the union, and I expect you to understand." And that is the way it ought to be.

A few of the newly elected leaders expressed attitudes like this:

> You know, I didn't even know what the general manager looked like before I joined the union, and now I sit right across from him two or three times a week. And when I talk he has to listen.

Such starry-eyed wonder is short-lived. But most leaders do gain considerable satisfaction from the fact that they can demand that management treat them as equals.

Social outlets   For the leaders, though not for the rank and file, the union is a social outlet. The leadership group usually develops into a clique. Even when there are sharp political differences in executive board and membership meetings, rival leaders frequently drive each other home, drink beer together, and exchange plant anecdotes. Even though they may quarrel bitterly with each other, they share a common "madness"—they are different from the rest.

But there are leaders who rarely "go out with the boys." When they do drink, they do so as a political obligation. For example:

> Am I glad these negotiations are over! The meetings were bad enough, three or four times a week, but what got me down was that I was forced to hang around with the gang until 1:00 or 2:00 in the morning. You don't want to look silly and drink coffee—so I'd have a sour stomach all the time.

Such men prefer to spend the time at home. For them, the union does offer a form of social satisfaction, although not the "buddy-buddy, backslapping" type. These less outgoing men look forward to the give-and-take of the executive committee meetings with considerable anticipation. Also, they seem to enjoy membership meetings (although not to the same extent). One explanation for this phenomenon might be that the executive board and most of the membership meeting participants are within the "clique," while most other meetings frequently include a large proportion of "outsiders."

A few of the active leaders engage in almost no informal social contacts; they rarely take part in the whispered conversation during membership meetings and executive board meetings. Some of these men suffer from emotional difficulties which make it hard for them to relax in an easy, friendly way. When such men get elected, it is to technical, time-consuming jobs like secretary or treasurer.

Of course, all these men frequently complain about how much they are overworked, how they would like to have spare time for themselves, how they are taken advantage of by the rank and file, and how they are not appreciated. But when they have a chance to get time off, they don't take it. Unionism casts a spell which is hard to break. "Big shots" stay at the office even when there is nothing to do. When one department is having a meeting, leaders from other departments will show up "just to give a hand," although in many cases this helping hand is strongly resented.

Relations with the Community

In most locals, the fact that a person is a union officer is not known to the community at large. Even in small towns, only the president of the local receives much personal publicity. Of course, the neighbors next door may know that a man is a union officer; but if they are unsympathetic to the union, this may make things difficult, particularly for his wife during a strike.

We found, too, that company advertisements accusing local officials of incompetence or unwillingness to serve the best interest of their members never go unheeded. Naturally, the officers are worried that such charges will be believed by at least a significant minority of their members.

Top officers, on the other hand, obtain some recognition from their community. The president may get publicity in the form of newspaper photographs or membership in the Community Chest. This is an increasing trend and gives them additional status and prestige. For the majority of leaders at the moment, however, the community offers no such rewards.

Participation in community activities   The fact that they are not recognized does not mean that the leaders withdraw from the community. In fact, our research shows just the opposite to be the case. Thus, in line with earlier observations about their high activity level, a heavy proportion of them are active members of outside community organizations. Tables 1 and 2 summarize illustrative statistics covering twenty-nine out of thirty-four officers and stewards from a "mature, well-Americanized" local (Local A) in a

Table 1 / Nonunion Organizations to Which Individual Union Leaders Belong

Number of Organizations	Local A Officers Belonging		Local B Officers Belonging	
	Number	Percentage	Number	Percentage
None	5	17	3	12
One	14	49	3	12
Two	4	14	10	40
Three	3	10	3	12
Four or More	3	10	6	24
	29	100	25	100

Table 2 / Pattern of Union Leaders' Organizational Membership*

	Number of Officers Belonging	
Type of Organization	Local A	Local B
Fraternal		
Knights of Columbus	6	2
Italian	0	6
Polish	0	7
Other	11	11
Religious	3	3
Political	7*	3
Athletic	4	3
Rifle and Conservation	0	4
Veterans	8	2
National Guard	3	0
Community Improvement	3	0
Volunteer Fireman	0	4
	45	45

* Three ran for office as well; one is now a member of his local school board.

large city and the major officers and stewards in an ethnically divided community of 25,000 (Local B). Both groups are overwhelmingly Catholic.

Our impression is that in most locals 60 to 90 per cent of the executive board members participate in outside organizations. At least a third attend meetings of one kind or another two or three nights a month. This compares with a probable figure of 40 to 50 per cent for working class membership in organizations generally.[1]

"Administrators" and "Social Leaders"

The discussion so far has been largely descriptive. We have tried to describe certain attitudes and behavior which appear to be common to the local leaders studied. The following, more analytical, section attempts to make distinctions within this officer group, and in so doing to suggest a possible explanation of these differences in terms of behavior within both the union and the larger community. In a preceding chapter, we attempted to divide stewards into three "ideal types" on the basis of their general orientation: the active unionist, the social leader, and the self-seeker. Somewhat the same approach may be applied to the local-wide officer.

The data show that these leaders are apparently of two types: the *administrator* and the *social leader*. The administrator is the top-officer equivalent of the active unionist. He sees his job as relating "outward" to the union's problems and its bargaining relationship with management.

The term "administrator" is used instead of "active unionist" in order to avoid confusion, for indeed the social-leader officer is just as loyal to the union, and spends as much time on local affairs, as the administrator. However, as in the case of his counterpart at the steward level, the social leader's primary interest is dealing with individuals rather than issues, personalities rather than abstractions.

None of the officers observed could be called a company man but, like most of their fellow men, many were interested in economic success—and they felt considerable conflict, particularly as to whether they should accept promotions into management jobs.

The "Administrator"

Union-wide officers who are administrators are often good executives and public-relations men. They are high in verbal skills, at least compared to the

[1] Cf., W. L. Warner and J. O. Low, *The Social System of the Modern Factory* (New Haven: Yale University Press, 1947).

W. L. Warner, *et al., Democracy in Jonesville* (New York: Harper & Row, 1949), p. 141.

M. Komarovsky, "The Voluntary Association of Urban Dwellers," *American Sociological Review*, Vol. 11, No. 6 (December 1946), pp. 686–698.

rank and file. When they speak in meetings, their English is good, their voices are well modulated, and what they have to say is carefully organized. They use profanity rarely—and then for carefully considered effect.

They are quick thinkers in debate and forceful advocates. They are effective on the meeting floor and equally so in negotiations with management.

Many union officers are tough fighters and know the contract through and through. But this combination of orneriness and intellect does not make for a successful social leader. The man who is smart enough to become an office manager and pugnacious enough to become a negotiator frequently is restless, driving, and, from the point of view of his fellow workers, overambitious.

Our research suggests that many of those who ranked high as administrators were relatively unpopular within their own work group. One officer slaved devotedly to make sure that every grievance was airtight. His services to the union were substantial, yet he had few friends in his own department. He, himself, confessed:

> I hardly know the men in my department. I am so busy with the union that I just don't have time to hang around with them . . . I don't think I am really a good leader. I am not as good as Jack Williams (an informal leader). But I am good on this administrative work.

In another case, an observer explained:

> Gus Spitzer hardly polls a vote among his own gang. They think he is a little bit too good for himself. But all the others see is that he runs around and takes their troubles for them. So he wins votes outside his department.

As discussed before, the men who make successful union leaders have a surplus of energy and ambition. Their fellow workers often find them too nervous and jittery to make comfortable companions. Perhaps, indeed, many of these men become active in the union because of their failure to make friends among their work associates. In any case, many union-wide officers spend so much time on their duties that they have little opportunity for idly "shooting the breeze" with their fellow workers.

The "Social Leader"

Contrasted with administrators are the social leaders. The amount of time and energy they devote to union activities attests to their loyalty and interest in the local. Still, since their primary interest is in individuals rather than their problems, they are much more like ward leaders than statesmen.

One such local president was a poor presiding officer; he couldn't keep order and regularly made parliamentary errors. He left all his office work to his secretary and constantly had to be rescued during grievance and contract negotiations. Yet he was popular with the rank and file and usually blundered through to an acceptable decision. The president of another local was generally considered to be stubborn in collective bargaining. This seemed to be his chief asset, as he was ineffective as a chairman and pathetically timid as a speaker. Although his supporters admitted that he wasn't "very sharp," somehow they made this into almost a virtue:

> You may say this about Tim, he's as honest as the day is long. The men trust him because he's not better than they are.

The vice-president of another local sat three months in contract negotiations and never uttered a word. Except when he had to assume the chair, he was equally silent during ten months of membership meetings. Although he lacked sufficient local-wide popularity to win re-election, his own work group turned out meeting after meeting to give him support.

Will Johnson may be typical of the social leader. In addition to his widespread union activities, Will took a prominent part in the local Democratic organization. However, he constantly refused to run for political office, saying:

> If I were elected for something I'd be obligated to people. Right now, I can do favors for everybody, not because I expect returns—but because that's the greatest pleasure of my life. Why it's wonderful, everybody knows me. The politicians, the garbage man, the teacher, the kids in the street, they all know me and say, "Hi, Will."

This same love of personal contact was carried over to the union. While many other officers would brag of their victories against the company, Will spoke of the large number of people he saw daily and the regard they had for him.

Thus we can picture two types of individuals. The administrator, who is technically proficient but perhaps not too popular among his fellow workers. The social leader is a poor meeting chairman and inefficient at drawing up grievances, yet as an informal leader, generally trusted and well liked by the members.

Within the administrator group, a further subdivision can be made. A majority seems anxious to "get ahead"; they have "upward status aspirations." But there is a smaller group which seems to reject respectability almost deliberately. It consists of men who have been brought up in economically well-to-do families and, through adversities, have been thrown into the labor movement. These officers are often the most aggressively antimanagement of all.

Typical of this latter group, was the son of a prominent doctor. This man had gone through college and was attending graduate school when a family crisis forced him to quit. He obtained an industrial job in a nearby plant and has worked there ever since, devoting his energies and abilities entirely to the union. He holds himself aloof from his fellow workers in the shop, but is extraordinarily adept at gathering and processing data for bargaining sessions. He belongs to no outside organizations, but he averages eight hours a day on union business in addition to his working hours in the plant! His wife, however, is active in a fashionable church. He always wears white shirts and expensive ties, but they are not kept clean. There were men like him in other locals studied, but this group was always in the minority.

Most administrators seemed to look upon the union as a chance to get ahead and as a socially acceptable opportunity to be aggressive against those elements of a "system" which they felt had relegated them to an inferior position.

Thus, the union provides leadership opportunities for more than one type of personality. Leaders have varying motivations and act in different ways. Yet each type may perform an essential function for the union.

Conclusion

Our discussion has been descriptive rather than explanatory. We have tried to portray the local leader as he is, rather than to discover how he got to be that way. The latter is a more difficult process which would take us deep into the childhood experience of each individual.

It will be enough if we can shed some light on the inner dynamics of those who sit on the union side of collective-bargaining tables. Our evidence suggests that the personality which makes an effective union leader is little different from that which makes an aggressive, able business executive. The position of the union leader is somewhat more complicated, however, because he has two "jobs," one of which has more political overtones than the job of the average business bureaucrat.

Both have driving energy. Both are dissatisfied with the status quo. Each gets satisfaction from tackling his environment and trying his best to mold it to his liking. Both get into trouble with their families, because they spend too much time at "work." Certainly both are "joiners," and both are equally anxious to get ahead in the world, although "getting ahead" may be measured by different yardsticks.

8

The Selection of Union Officers

This chapter will consider primarily two questions: First, what are the *issues* in union elections? What do the candidates say they support, and even more significantly, what are the underlying sources of rank-and-file discontent which can affect election results? Second, from what jobs in the plant are leaders selected? These questions are interrelated.

Our thesis is this: when the membership is reasonably satisfied with its general working conditions and level of earnings, officers will tend to be selected from those holding high-status jobs. However, general rank-and-file discontent may result in economic questions becoming vital issues in election campaigns, with a consequent widespread turnover in the administration. When this occurs, the new leaders often come from lower-status jobs than did the previous officeholders. After the crest of the reform wave has passed, a higher-status group often returns to control.

The Issues

Common sense would suggest that since unions are concerned primarily with collective bargaining, union elections would be fought primarily over collective-bargaining issues—over how militant a stand to take against management or over how to divide the fruits of bargaining among competing interest groups. Yet, we seldom observed the issues so sharply joined. The voter was rarely in a position to select between real alternative objectives. On the contrary, just as in national political struggles, there was much more mudslinging than discussion of issues. Each side claimed that it could do better—but almost no one was specific as to the exact changes of existing policy he would make or the type of new policies he would introduce.

Why do candidates neglect these collective-bargaining issues? One obvious reason is their general unwillingness to campaign for lesser benefits. Except in the case of periods of extreme economic hardship, when the firm faces bankruptcy, no candidate would conceive of criticizing his opponent for asking too much. Conflict between competing interest groups rarely offers a campaign issue because, with significant exceptions (e.g., day workers vs. night workers), such conflicts involve relatively small numbers of members, who work close to each other. Although the conflicts are very important to the men concerned, they engage relatively few individuals in any given dispute. As a rule, they are confined within the department, or departments, concerned. They may affect department-wide elections, but rarely become open issues in union-wide politics. In many industries, the International plays a key role in the negotiation of wage rates, thus taking the issue out of the hands of the local officers.

Furthermore, in a reasonably large plant it is hard for a worker to evaluate plant-wide candidates in terms of small-group self-interest. Specific campaign promises are extremely rare in union election campaigns. As a consequence, a worker in the machine shop has no idea how the presidential candidate from the shipping room feels about his seniority dispute with another machinist over a promotion.

General Upheavals

Lincoln Steffens pointed out that municipal conditions must be really bad before the voters rise up to "kick the rascals out." The same holds true for local unions. General upheavals, when economic dissatisfaction leads to a widespread change of officers, are the exception. But they happen under at least three types of circumstances: (1) when the members feel that their economic conditions have worsened because of inefficient or insufficiently militant officers; (2) when serious collective-bargaining differences arise (over how to divide the pie) which split the entire local; and (3) when a large number of departments are frustrated over small, individual problems which have somehow coalesced.

Insufficient or ineffective militancy   General frustration may develop throughout the local because of the feeling that the officers have not been able to win gains as great as those obtained by other unions. Union members are well aware of the prevailing pattern, and if they get less than this they may cause trouble.

Such was the case in a union which held a two-year contract providing for wage reopening after one year, with disagreement to be settled by arbitration. The reopening period came just after the company's major competitor had given an increase of 10 cents an hour. In the case under consideration, the arbitrator awarded only 4 cents. The ensuing election was a turbulent one, and the incumbents were swept out.

Differences between interest groups   In some instances, differences between union-wide interest groups (such as skilled and unskilled workers) affect union-wide elections.

One case involved a dispute between incentive and day-rate workers. During the war years, the earnings of the incentive workers far outstripped those of day workers of higher skill. This condition smoldered for six years while the officers promised that something would be done. Finally, when a newly negotiated contract failed to provide adequate adjustments, the day workers united for the first time and elected a completely new slate to the negotiating committee.

Similarly, maladjustments in the plant wage structure, such as those resulting from cents-per-hour or across-the-board rather than percentage wage increases, have been observed to affect elections.

Combination of smaller issues   Incidental dissatisfactions of small groups may add up. Each department may have its own minor cause for unhappiness, but the total may be enough to upset the administration. When this happens, it is almost impossible for either observer or participants to give explanations. Totally unpredicted "election flukes" may occur; almost complete unknowns may be elected as a protest against the incumbent.

In one plant, dissatisfaction with the incumbent leadership because of inequities in the wage structure, a lengthy strike to help another union, and failure to include a broader representation of the ethnic groups in the plant, did not crystallize into any serious opposition for six years. Finally, a petty seniority dispute affecting one individual precipitated a major turnover of the officers.

This problem existed in the wage-reopener case discussed above, with the arbitration award serving as the precipitating factor. Each department received the same small wage increase, but some were more upset about it than others. Every department which voted strongly against the administration had its own cause for complaint. Some objected to the inequities in job evaluation, others to the way their grievances had been sidetracked, and so forth. Thus, by the time the arbitration award was handed down, many of the departments were convinced that the union leadership was "selling out to management." The award was only the final bit of evidence they required.

Even in cases like these the real economic issue is often disguised. The members feel they want a change but cannot identify the source of their dissatisfactions. Instead, they may look upon the fighting merely as a question of rival personalities, of poor administration, or of ideological differences.

The fact that rank-and-file members are primarily interested in "bread and butter" issues is shown in the results of various ideological fights which have developed over the "Commie" issue in the left-wing-controlled unions. In case after case, right-wing leaders have found that patriotic appeals to the membership to overthrow their Communist domination have fallen on deaf ears as long as political questions were emphasized. Effective results were obtained only when it could be proved that Communist leaders had "frittered away" the union's strength on political issues, rather than winning collective-bargaining gains.

Although we have listed a number of situations where economic issues play an important part in union elections, it should be emphasized that these are more or less exceptional. Indeed, in many locals disputed elections of any kind are rare, and local-wide officers are re-elected unanimously.

When there *is* a contest, local-wide elections are conducted with considerable ballyhoo and all the trappings of an American political campaign. There are distributions of circulars, wild charges, mudslinging, campaign stunts, and all the rest. Vituperative personal attacks fly back and forth. The "ins" point with pride, the "outs" view with alarm. The ins are accused of being too conservative, the outs of wrecking and irresponsibility. Each charges the other with playing into the company's hands.

Much of the sound and fury, however, signifies nothing more than the personal ambitions of one active union member conflicting with those of another. In none of the cases observed, were there hard and fast "party systems." Candidates for different offices would often arrange temporary alliances, but these as a rule were based on expediency rather than principle.

Election Issues Within the Small Group

Since intraunion disputes over economic issues are far more common *within* small, face-to-face groups, we should expect that elections for steward (the chief officer elected by the small group) should be hot contests over clearly defined collective-bargaining questions. Actually, just the opposite occurs. In most unions, stewards must be recruited. When election fights do occur, they are far less lively than those on the local-wide level.

Why are there so few contests for the steward office? This would seem to be the result of three factors:

1. As mentioned earlier, the steward's job is not often considered desirable. The steward gets all the "dirty work" and little of the glory or the satisfaction from actually making decisions. For this reason it often becomes difficult to find a single candidate for the job, let alone two who will compete.

2. Although workers have many complaints, only rarely do they perceive the changing of stewards as a means of improving conditions. In most instances, the job is not important enough to get excited over. In a previous chapter, we listed various forms of pressure available to discontented groups: they can file grievances, buttonhole officers, attend meetings, or engage in self-help activities such as wildcat strikes or restriction of output. Many of these are viewed as much more effective measures than changing a steward—particularly if the office is almost powerless.

3. The general atmosphere which surrounds stewardship elections is such as to discourage making them into as much of a "game" as local-wide elections. The bare mechanics of the stewardship election play an important role in this. The union-wide election is relatively formalized. Even if there is no high-pressure campaigning (with literature and the rest), the elections are held at well-publicized times and places. In almost all circumstances, secret ballots are used. In a sense, this depersonalizes the fight.

Stewardship elections are normally far more informal—sometimes they are not held at all. The usual procedure is for one of the local officers to gather the men in the department together (in the plant, bar or lunchroom outside, or perhaps in the union hall) and ask them to choose whom they want. The decision often is unanimous, and disagreements, if any, are settled by a show of hands.

Such informal procedure inhibits real opposition. As one man said, just before having to cast a standing vote in a disputed election:

> This is going to be very embarrassing. I think O'Connor deserves the job. But Lovell is a friend of mine and I hate to stand up against him.

This results in the atmosphere of the shop election being considerably different from one on the local-wide level.

The union-wide leaders seem to enjoy squabbling with each other. Stewardship elections resemble more a family quarrel than a formal contest for office. The parties are too close to make the issue a game. Under most circumstances, the parties preserve their politeness. Thus, there are important social constraints which prevent a worker from making too much of a "fuss." If Bill has been a steward for a number of years, the average worker will think Frank's efforts to unseat him in poor taste.

The Candidates

Taking the locals we have studied as a whole, only rarely did young, low-paid workers hold key positions in the local. On the contrary, in most cases a large proportion of the officers elected were: (1) higher-paid and more skilled workers; (2) workers with more seniority, both within the plant and within the union; (3) workers who had ample chance to talk and to move around the plant; (4) from dominant ethnic groups; and (5) men rather than women. (These last two aspects are considered in Chapter 12.) All these factors relate to "status" or social prestige.

Pay Rate and Status

Our research indicates a general tendency for union leaders to be selected from among the higher-paid and more highly skilled workers. Union-wide officers often hold the highest-paid jobs under the jurisdiction of the local; stewards frequently are the highest paid in their department.[1]

In one company, thirteen of seventeen officers were at the top of their promotional ladders. The president was in the highest pay grade, with only eight others out of 1,800 receiving as much as he.

Table 3, which summarizes the results of elections in one union for a five-year period, shows that, although only 28 per cent of the work force received in excess of $63 a week (in terms of 1950 pay), 60 per cent of the votes were cast for men in this pay grade.

This company, with approximately 2,000 employees, has its operations spread over a wide area and divided among three shifts. As a result, the opportunity for workers to compare each other's jobs is limited.

An automobile assembly plant is a relatively compact unit. It is easy for an aspiring politician to get to know many people. The vast majority of the workers are doing roughly the same kind of job, and comparisons between merits of jobs are simple to make. Table 4 gives data from two such plants, each with approximately 1,500 employees. In Plant A, five out of eight offices were contested. The election in Plant B was quite turbulent, with sharp fights for each position and as many as six candidates for some offices. In fact, the

Table 3 / Distribution of Vote According to Candidates' Pay Grades

Weekly Wage	Percentage of Workers in Given Pay Grades	Percentage of Votes Cast for Candidates in Given Pay Grades
$71.50 or more	3	14
$67.00–70.50	11	16
$63.00–66.50	14	30
$55.00–62.50	34	32
$48.00–54.50	19	7
$47.50 and under	19	1
	100	100

[1] Many unions make a strenuous attempt to get a "balanced slate" of officers through getting representatives from many departments. To some extent, this "distribution" of officers obscures the concentration of real control.

president's margin of victory was only 2 per cent. Forty per cent of the workers voted in Plant A and 85 per cent in Plant B.

In Plant A, the successful candidates for president and the chairman of the grievance committee were tool-and-die makers, both receiving the highest rate paid any union occupation in the plant. Candidates from departments having 6 per cent of the labor force received 45 per cent of the votes. On the other hand, assemblers, who comprised a large portion of the total work force, had far less than proportional representation in terms of votes received and officers elected.

For organizational purposes the union divided Plant B into three sections having equal membership: (1) maintenance, body build, and parts; (2) trim; and (3) chassis. The jobs in the first category carried the highest prestige—that is, were the most highly desired—and the second and third followed in descending order. It is revealing to observe, that two-thirds of the votes were cast for men who worked in Group 1, while no officer was elected from Group 3, and therefore an executive board member had to be assigned

Table 4 / Results of Elections in Two Plants According to Pay Grades of Those Elected

		Plant A			Plant B*		
	Hourly Pay Range	% of Workers	Per Cent Votes Received	No. of Officers	% of Workers	Per Cent Votes Received	No. of Officers Elected
Tool and Die	$1.82–2.06	1	27	2	—†	—	—
Skilled Maintenance	$1.78–1.98	5	18	1	7	16	3
Materials Handling (Stock Room)	$1.47–1.52	12	0	0	9	32	4
Inspector	$1.52–1.65	5	5	1	3	8	1
Truck Driver	$1.57	1	0	0	1	6	1
Semi-skilled Production‡	$1.57–1.82	32	40	4	2	30	1
Unskilled production (Assemblers, etc.‡)	$1.47–1.56	41	10	0	71	8	1
Unskilled Maintenance	$1.32–1.62	3	0	0	7	0	0
		100	100	8	100	100	11

* The pay range in Plant B is not available. However, it is believed to be roughly equivalent to that in Plant A, except for stock and tool room clerks.
† No such classification in union.
‡ It is not clear whether the significantly different distributions of those assigned to "skilled" and "unskilled" categories in the two plants reflect real differences in technology.

to represent them. (This officer in turn objected strongly that he was being "degraded.")

In several needle trades locals, cutters and pressers were the highest paid workers in the industry. Among them they held almost all the top offices, although they comprised but 30 per cent of the membership. In the election for the two business agents, one was called the "cutters' agent" and the other the "pressers' agent." It was felt that only the cutters and pressers had a chance to be elected, although occasionally operators and miscellaneous workers made futile attempts.

Lower-paid workers are sometimes completely unrepresented. In one manufacturing plant, the coalheavers were without a steward of their own, although many smaller groups had separate representation. The steward who had jurisdiction over them made no reference to their grievances until directly questioned by the interviewer, when he said, "Oh, yes, I'm in charge of them too, but they don't cause me any trouble." When asked how he found out what their grievances were, since he worked in a different part of the plant, he said, "Well, I suppose they'd get a message to me somehow. I don't know—it hasn't come up yet."

Seniority

Seniority and age are almost as important as pay in determining a worker's chance of being elected to union office. In a majority of cases, the discrimination against younger or lower-seniority employees is due to a feeling that they have had less experience or merely that they are "young upstarts." Superseniority—which permits younger officers to keep their jobs when older nonofficers are laid off—provokes comments like this one by a local president:

> The guys don't like this superseniority, so they get around it by always electing the oldest man as steward. The duds we get this way! Now you understand why I have to handle all the grievances myself.

Communications Opportunities

Wherever there is rivalry for office a given candidate's chances for success depend to a considerable extent upon his communications opportunities. Even if a man holds a high-prestige job, we must ask further: Can he talk to others? Can others see him? Can he move around? How far? Other things being equal, those who have the greatest chance to talk to others are most likely to become leaders. As an officer remarked:

> To tell you the truth, I spend most of my time talking. To be sure, I go around from place to place inspecting [as required by his company job]— I let nothing dangerous happen. But this is the time I build the union.

In one company, three of the five top union officers had roving jobs which carried them all over the plant. The other two were supposedly tied to their jobs, but actually they too spent a large part of their working hours talking to other members.

In a white-collar local, office machine operators were frequently elected as stewards or officers. Their job had a high political potential for three reasons: (1) they were in constant contact with the clerks who brought them material to process; (2) while the machines were operating they had ample time to talk with anyone in the vicinity; (3) in many of the offices they were the only men present.

As a rule, maintenance and supply men have unusual political advantages, although for opposite reasons. Maintenance men move around from worker to worker, while the workers themselves are required to visit the supply clerks.

Shipping and receiving, a department whose function was close to that of supply, played a key political role in a medium-sized chemical plant. This department was located in the very center of the main building. Although the president of the union was a maintenance man, the vice-president, the treasurer, and the sergeant-at-arms were all shippers.

It must be emphasized again that communication is no more a single determining factor than any of the others so far discussed. To make this clear, let us take the example of the cleaners in a large manufacturing plant. These workers acted as a communications link between departments. They carried rumors, information, and messages as part of their jobs, and so were looked upon as people who "knew what was up." In spite of this, none was ever elected or ran for office. It would seem that the low pay and menial nature of their job made their status entirely too low for successful political ambition.

Analysis

In all but two of the situations studied, the bulk of the officers and stewards came from the highest-paid 20 per cent of the work group. Other factors such as communications position, seniority, sex, and nationality further narrowed the groups from which the majority of officers were selected. A few hypotheses which may explain this selection of higher-status workers follow.

1. High-prestige groups are more likely to participate in union activities (see Chapter 11). Assuming that they support their "favorite sons," these will have a better chance to win elections than those of lower-prestige groups.

2. To some extent, individuals holding high-status jobs are more likely to win votes since they are "respectable" or "looked up to" by other members of the work community. It may be that a rank-and-file member thinks that a man who has not been successful on his job is not a good bet as a union officer. The stereotype held unconsciously by the rank and file as to what makes

a good officer may include elements relating to pay, seniority, ethnic background, sex, etc.

3. In general, one may expect that a high-status worker would be unlikely to want a lower-status worker as his leader. On the other hand, a lower-status worker might show less resistance to being represented by someone with higher status.

4. Many of the higher-paid jobs require quasi-supervisory duties and human-relations skills. In many instances, men who are successful at these jobs provide good officer material.

5. Similarly, longer-service employees usually have exhibited some competence in dealing with day-to-day interpersonal problems. Those who cannot adjust often leave the plant or keep transferring from department to department and miss out on opportunities to establish strong ties with fellow workers and to promote themselves politically.

Deviations from this pattern may well provide additional insights into the election process. The cases described below are typical of those we observed. However, since they cover only newly formed locals, they probably are not representative of all the various instances in which low- or middle-status workers gain control of the local.

Defeat of an independent union   For a period of eight years the C.I.O. and an independent union were locked in a bitter struggle for the allegiance of employees in a large manufacturing plant. The C.I.O. charged the independent with being insufficiently aggressive in seeking pay raises and better promotions and its officers with "selling out to management." Their opponents argued that the introduction of a national union would "just cause trouble." Rumors were circulated about the evil effects of "outside domination" by the "Communist" C.I.O. The C.I.O. lost three elections in a row, but finally won on its fourth try.

To some extent, the contest was between higher- and lower-paid workers. An aggressive C.I.O. leader pointed out:

> The best men to contact are men just starting out, still ambitious, beginning to realize that they aren't going to make a million. The most difficult to organize are those on the top. But when things settle down, they make good leaders.

The first elections under the C.I.O. saw the center of political power move sharply downwards on the pay scale. The old president came from one of the highest pay groups, the new one from one of the lowest. In recent elections under the independent, candidates from the top pay brackets received 15 per cent of the total vote cast. Under the new union this group received less than 1 per cent of the vote.

Eighty-five per cent of the new officers and stewards had not held office under the independent. Many of the independent officers had held quasi-supervisory jobs. The members now felt that these men were "too close to the top." "Lead men" and inspectors similarly were thought to be "tainted" with management.

Within eighteen months after control of the union had shifted to the lower-status workers, there were definite signs of a movement back to the older "equilibrium." Low-paid officers were being replaced by higher-paid ones. In six of the eight officer elections for which there was a serious contest, the highest-paid candidate was successful. Indeed, the first president of the C.I.O. was replaced by the former president of the independent! In the first election under the C.I.O., officers in the two highest wage grades received something less than 20 per cent of the votes; they received 31 per cent in the second election. This compares with 30 per cent received by the same group during the independent period.

A steel plant Late in 1941 the C.I.O. organized a medium-sized basic steel mill after a sharp struggle. The drive was spearheaded by unskilled, comparatively low-paid men from the fabricating department. The first two presidents were fabricators, earning "Job Class 8" pay (Job Class 30 was the highest-paid). After five years, control shifted to the steelmaking departments, which elected both the third president (Job Class 18) and the incumbent (Job Class 24).

A quality furniture company In a furniture plant, organized by the C.I.O. during the middle of World War II, the majority of the union's officers and its organizational strength came from the unskilled departments. Although the union obtained substantial wage increases, these were primarily of the cents-per-hour type which tended to decrease traditional differentials between skilled groups.

An A.F.L. union began working with the skilled groups, relying heavily on the Communist issue. In the National Labor Relations Board election that followed, the A.F.L. won—but by a small margin. Although the A.F.L. shop committee was elected in the same manner as that of the C.I.O. that preceded it, all the top officers of the new union held skilled jobs. The first new A.F.L. contract granted percentage wage increases that widened the pay gap between unskilled and skilled workers and actually *reduced* the minimum wage rate that could be paid in the plant.

Conclusion

Let us tie the preceding material together with the object of presenting a dynamic picture of the selection process:

Under "normal conditions" (when the officers are not engaging in blatant maladministration and the workers are not too dissatisfied with their working conditions), workers with high status will hold many of the important positions within the union. To the rank and file, these men *are* the union. They are held responsible for all the union does. Although the rank and file may feel some hostility toward the officers, this is balanced by inertia.

Except in periods of "revolt," election battles will be fought largely over personalities and ethnic differences. Even though a large proportion of the members may vote, their interest is superficial, and issues are not weighed nor are platforms scrutinized seriously.

Worker dissatisfaction with the way the union is being run may arise from a number of conditions: (1) a feeling that the officers are insufficiently aggressive—or (rarely) too aggressive; (2) a series of economic reverses, for which the officers are the scapegoats; (3) a combination of frustrations arising in many small groups; (4) a belief that the officers are favoring certain special interest groups (such as nightworkers or pieceworkers); or (5) a conviction that the officers are dishonest or self-seeking.

If there is enough dissatisfaction, members may shift from passive resignation to a feeling that "something should be done about it." This dissatisfaction may be expressed in a number of ways: sitdown strikes, attendance at meetings, grievances, absenteeism, or even a change in union affiliation. If this discontent crystallizes around election time, there may then be a drastic turnover in officers.

Relative prestige rarely enters elections as a verbalized issue. The real differences are those of apparent aggressiveness—the young against the old, the new champions against the worn-out veterans. The new administration is elected chiefly because of resentment against the old. The incoming officers are often drawn from lower-status groups primarily because those with higher status are too closely connected with the old, rejected leadership. On occasion, if an "untainted" high-status group is available, it may well provide the new officers. However, higher-paid workers are more susceptible to suspicions of a "management taint"—they appear *too* successful to make aggressive leaders.

Control by lower- and middle-status groups will not last long. Once the crisis is over, leadership will slowly shift back to higher-status groups—if for no other reason than that the new leaders themselves grow older, acquire seniority, and get promoted. While the shift downward (to control by lower-status group) may assume the form of a dramatic revolt, a shift upward will more likely occur through a gradual process of replacement.

9

Conflict and Unity on the Executive Board

Although previous chapters have described the relations of local-wide officers to the membership and management, little attention has been given to their relations to one another.

Most officers thrive on debate. There is seemingly no end of subjects for dispute and the patience of the participants never seems to wane. They debate often over seemingly minor questions: How much of an executive committee meeting must a member sit through before he is entitled to supper money? Should the chairman of a new committee be elected or appointed by the president? What should be the authority of one officer relative to that of another?

Bickering and factionalism within the top officer group is also an evident feature of the union scene, and there is a constantly changing pattern of alliances. One day two leaders may be exchanging support and mending each other's fences; the next day they may be sworn enemies. Much of the politicking and bloc formation involves competition for "prestige jobs" such as convention delegate or membership on the contract negotiations committee. Although the remuneration for most union offices is hardly enough to cover out-of-pocket costs, being a convention delegate or taking part in multiplant negotiations involves an interesting all-expense-paid trip, as well as a chance to meet people from other locals and the almost legendary figures from the International.

Many of the disputes arise out of the clashing personalities and political ambitions of the participants. Ethnic differences, too, fan the flames. Board members' votes, as will later be shown, are often affected by ethnic prejudice.

Around election time there is a strong tendency for local union politics to enter into grievance handling. Officers become far more receptive to questionable cases than they are at other times of the year. During executive board meetings the charges fly that one faction or the other is stealing all the "easy" cases—or, contrariwise, pushing irresponsible complaints which the union can never hope to win. And, with considerable justification, it is often alleged that certain officers are favoring those departments in which they have the greatest political strength.

Intergroup Disputes

The emphasis given earlier to intergroup disputes might lead one to predict that this would be an important source of conflict among top officers. But this is not the case. Although the executive board is often divided as to how a grievance should be handled, the arguments are usually not related to the departmental affiliation of specific members of the board.

In general, the officers take a rather judicial or legalistic point of view toward disputes between rival groups. In some instances, officers even disqualify themselves from considering problems affecting their own department. By and large, the executive board's approach to grievance handling is dispassionate—at least compared to their handling of matters of "internal politics."

Radicals and Conservatives

Some of the sharpest and longest-lasting disputes within the executive board take place between *radicals* and *conservatives*. As used in shop parlance, these terms do not have a political meaning. Radicals are those who want to push every grievance to the hilt, while conservatives feel that a more tactful approach will pay greater dividends. Their conflict is not over the merits of particular grievances, but over the question of how hard they should be pushed.

Conservatives are, for the most part, older, higher-paid men. As suggested in Chapter 8 they dominate the union, except when economic stress or some other crisis has resulted in a turnover. These men are not adverse to direct action when clearly necessary. Still, by temperament, they would prefer to reach their goals through peaceful, businesslike bargaining. They are proud of their personal relationships developed with individual management representatives and are anxious to hold the respect of both the company and the community.

These men are fully aware of intergroup differences and of the need to maintain the local's unity. They realize that indiscriminate espousal of all grievances incurs many risks. For these reasons, they seek to restrain over-aggressive young hotheads from pushing individual cases so fast as to jeopardize the local's over-all progress.

The typical extreme radicals have been newly elected to office: the longer they hold office the more conservative most of them become. In general, they hold lower-status jobs or come from groups seeking greater political importance in the local. Often they belong to ethnic minorities and are smarting from actual or imagined discrimination.

Frequently, the radical feels that he has been elected with a mandate to clean house. He charges the conservatives with an indifference to management tyranny and a hunger for personal power. He looks upon the growing trend toward centralization within the grievance procedure as a threat to the union's democratic vigor. The radical argues that many of the union's troubles can be traced to the failure to maintain the lower steps of the grievance procedure (although in his own department he is as likely to by-pass the steward as those he accuses). He is anxious to harass and annoy the company wherever possible and is particularly suspicious of attempts to "sell out" the contract, which he holds sacred, by informal agreements.

The informal bargaining technique is particularly vulnerable to attack. The radicals can appeal to the rank-and-file level and thereby threaten the strategic position of the top bargaining team. The radical is usually able to point to some secret agreement which has "soured"—because it has worked out poorly in practice or perhaps because conditions have changed. This can easily be called a "sellout."

The radicals' platform is one of firm resistance to management. Either because of inexperience or by design, they choose to ignore internal union differences which make some grievances mutually contradictory.

Such men create difficult problems for the conservatives, who look upon informal agreements with management as essential to maintaining adequate flexibility. One such troublemaker was Bill Sorgum. He was a real table-pounder who believed that every complaint should be pushed to the bitter end. Management resented his tactics. Although the Personnel manager got along easily with other officers, he fairly bristled every time Sorgum entered the conference room. It finally got to the point where the other officers refused to have Sorgum present during negotiations, for they found that once a case got into his hands it would take months to obtain a settlement. Of course, Sorgum took the positions that the company was retaliating for his militancy and that the others should support him.

Cohesive Forces

Bitter as the radical-conservative conflict may be, effort is often made to keep it within the closed circle of top officers. Of course, where splits are serious and long-lasting, the minority may marshal support in the plant for an eventual appeal to the membership meeting. Instances of this are rare and dramatic.

Executive committee meetings often start in a flurry of recriminations and ill feeling which sometimes last for two hours or more. When the members seem to have exhausted their antagonisms they settle down to work. Indeed, from a psychological point of view, it seems that these family quarrels within the privacy of the executive board room serve the function of catharsis; they give the officers a chance to get rid of pent-up frustrations and aggressions.

As we have seen, the officers are subject to conflicting pressures of all kinds. Rank-and-file members constantly approach them with grievances, many of which are unjustified, but all of which, they say, require the utmost dispatch in handling. The leader, at the same time, realizes that if he is to prosecute successfully any grievances he must exercise restraints in his relations with management. The officer, acting as a buffer between the rank and file and management, builds up tensions and has little chance to release them except when he is in the presence of his brother officers. This doubtless explains some of the wild accusations made within the confines of the executive board room.

Yet some of these very pressures which cause the officers to explode at each other in private also encourage them to maintain the semblance of a united front in public. As Muste puts it: the union is in one sense a military organization, and open airing of differences would aid the enemy.[1] Officers often say, "Here we are fighting among ourselves when we should be fighting the company," or "They [the company] are anxious to have us fight because they know that weakens us." Even conservatives, on occasion, welcome the activities of radicals, "when they really are getting in the hair of the company."

The officers stand together for still another reason. Regardless of how strenuously they may battle each other, common interests and experience give them some sense of unity. Even though they may argue, the argument is part of the game—and, like rivals in an athletic contest, they feel closer to their opponents than they do to outsiders.

Furthermore, they realize: "The members don't bother to distinguish between one union leader and another. As far as they are concerned, we are all alike." An attack by one officer or another can easily backfire and hurt

---

[1] A. J. Muste, "Factional Fights in Trade Unions," In *American Labor Dynamics,* J. B. S. Hardman, Ed. (New York: Harcourt, Brace & World, 1928), pp. 332–333.

them all. If one officer makes a mistake, all are blamed. The very ease of retaliation introduces a note of restraint into their political battles.

Conclusion

The factional fighting in the executive board gives an officer a chance to release some of his frustrations. Of course, many factional fights reach the floor of the union meeting; others are argued in the locker rooms and at the workbenches. But in general union leaders keep their differences "in bounds."

Factions there are, but these change with kaleidoscopic frequency. Only rarely are full-fledged party splits developed. On one issue the officers may cleave along radical-conservative lines, on another according to nationality, on a third according to attitudes toward expenditure of union funds. Further, the officers as individuals are changing as they grow in experience and perspective. All these prevent the development of a real party system.

There are other positive forces which give the officer group a feeling of unity. They are all in the same boat—they are all equally subject to attack by management or by the rank and file. And finally, although each one may have his personal political ambitions, almost all are devoted to the ideal of unionism. Although they may disagree as to how the union should be run, they agree as to their fundamental objective.

10

The Local Meeting: Its Functions and Problems

In recent years there has been a growing interest in union democracy. The local union is the basic building block of the union, and the local meeting, in theory, is the sovereign assembly which governs its affairs. Low attendance at meetings has been a subject of much concern outside as well as inside the union movement. Critics of union democracy point to the small minority who do attend as sensational proof that these organizations are not controlled by their membership. Union officers themselves are seriously worried that membership interest is drying up when meetings are held in empty halls. Some feel sure that management knows of this and interprets poor attendance as meaning that the officers have no support from the rank and file.

This chapter will provide (1) an over-all description of the meeting, with emphasis on the factors which discourage attendance, (2) an analysis of the motivation of those who attend, and (3) a general discussion of the functions actually performed by union meetings—especially decision-making.

The Meeting

Time and place Practically every local finds it hard to select a meeting time which will meet general approval. This is particularly difficult where the members' homes are scattered over a large city. If the meeting is held immediately after work, only a minimum amount of business can be transacted before suppertime. But if it is held after supper or on a weekend, only a handful of members are willing to leave the comfort of their homes and make the long trip to the meeting hall. Many members have commitments to other organizations which interfere with their union meeting attendance.

Shift operations introduce special problems. Our experience showed that the turnout at special meetings for night-shift workers was often proportionately as great as at the "regular" ones. However, the leaders thought these special meetings an unsatisfactory solution, since few of them could attend both shift and regular sessions.

Although the situation is improving, many meeting halls are still dirty and unattractive. Women in particular object to halls littered with soft-drink bottles and dusty piles of old union literature. Unfortunately, treasuries are limited and attractive halls expensive, particularly near the plants where most unions want to meet.

Length and content Many meetings start too late and last too long. It seems to be a well-established tradition in the labor movement for meetings to start from thirty to forty-five minutes late. Even more significant is their reputation for "lasting until all hours at night." The meetings observed averaged two hours in length, although some went on for four hours.

The contents of the meeting may discourage attendance as much as its length. The treasurer and financial secretary often give elaborate reports:

> Brother Chemski, $5.00 for a wreath; $16.16 lost time to Brother Smith, (eight hours at $2.02, his standard hourly wage) for work on the grievance in Department Z on January 16 and 17; $.96 postage; $120 office secretary for January; $37.84 withholding taxes and social security . . .

Financial secretaries, as a rule, are extremely sensitive to accusations of impropriety, and resist all attempts to reduce the amount of detail.

Many locals require that all "communications" received during the month be read to the membership. This means that the members must listen to countless pleas for charitable contributions and detailed administrative instructions from International headquarters. Often these take fifteen or twenty minutes to read. One recording secretary lamented, "We're on every sucker list in the country."

A large portion of the meeting is taken up by reports from the chairman of the executive board (often the president or the vice-president) and from whoever is most directly responsible for handling grievances and negotiations with management (either the business agent, where such exists, or the chairman of a grievance-bargaining committee).

In theory, the members must listen to these reports quietly. In practice, this is the point where the fireworks usually begin. Many members attend just to hear the discussion of their own grievances and to make interruptions, most of which are irrelevant from a strictly parliamentary point of view. This often makes the reading and discussion of the reports last well over an hour. Thus, "new business" (when the rank and file may bring up problems) may not be reached until hours after the scheduled start of the meeting and must usually be rushed through because the group has become restless. As the meeting winds on, the members go home one by one. Indeed, it is common for only half the members to stay on till final adjournment.

Chairmen   The chairmen observed varied greatly in the manner in which they handled meetings. A few were universally conceded to be scrupulously fair and dignified. Others obviously lacked training and experience. A majority did conscientious jobs, yet were subject to rank-and-file criticism. Interestingly, this criticism was often inconsistent. Some felt that the chairman was too autocratic, others that he was too weak.

Chairmen themselves often commented on their difficulties. They felt they ran the risk of making a permanent enemy every time they called a man out of order. Yet, they were painfully conscious that the meetings were often disorganized and overly long.

Poor chairmanship can be partly overcome by better training. Certainly many unions are making efforts in this direction. Yet, it has a deeper root in the "split personality" of the president, who is both chief executive of the union and moderator of the meeting. This recalls the conflict of function suggested by Muste.[1] During most of the month he must act on his own initiative as commander of an army, in situations where success is determined entirely by the exercise of personal forcefulness, ingenuity, and ability. But during the meetings he is expected to be the impartial moderator of a democratic deliberative body—even when his policies are under attack. Such switches in role are hard to make and hard for the members to accept. At times, a member starts to criticize the president's "army leader" activities at the wrong point on the agenda and is then called out of order. It is easy for him to suspect that the president is not being impartial.

In the meetings observed, the general attitude of the rank and file did little to ease the dilemma. They seemed to want someone to "give the answers" yet they resented being "railroaded." The impression given was that they objected to being dictated to, but were lost when given too much freedom.

Parliamentary procedures   Excessive parliamentarianism is frequently a major problem. A union must do more than learn how to use rules; it must learn to keep rules from using the union. Too often members have got them-

---

[1] A. J. Muste, "Factional Fights in Trade Unions," In *American Labor Dynamics*, J. B. S. Hardman, Ed. (New York: Harcourt, Brace & World, 1928), pp. 333–334.

selves tied into interminable parliamentary knots, to the frustration of everyone concerned. These were instigated by members who insisted that things be done "right," even if it meant taking all night. For example:

> A white-collar local spent twenty minutes debating whether a special motion was required to approve the treasurer's report, or whether it was sufficient for the president to state, "If there are no corrections or additions, the report will stand as read."

Communists were not the only groups to take advantage of parliamentary rigmarole. The various factions in one new local studied quickly learned the advantages to be derived from the confusing motion "to reconsider" or "to table." In these difficulties, the union is not alone among democratic assemblies.

Parliamentary experts had good intentions. At times they felt that they were preventing raw deals, but more often it was a question of sheer love of the game: a chance to show off all they knew, a chance to trip others up.

Attempts to increase attendance   Locals have tried a variety of techniques to bolster attendance. Many regularly provide beer and sandwiches at the end of the meetings. This is moderately effective and does increase the conviviality of the meetings. But one local discovered:

> We had pretty good attendance, but some joker would always get up and move the meeting be adjourned almost as soon as we started. The meetings were short and sweet, but we got nothing done.

Another local tried showing movies. An officer commented:

> We can never hope to compete with the commercial movies, and why the hell do we have the members here anyway? It's serious business, not kid stuff. The men have come here for work.

Many locals in the retail and clothing industries provide fines for members who fail to attend a specified minimum number of meetings per year. When this is enforced, attendance increases, phenomenally. As a rule, however, there is great reluctance about adopting such stringent measures and even when they are "on the books" they are frequently not enforced. Other locals offer door prizes. These seem to have little effect.

Rewards, in the form of refreshments, and punishments, in the form of fines for lethargic members, seem to have some effect on increasing attendance—but little on increasing interest.

Many members feel that union meetings are long, boring, and frustrating affairs. The following remark is typical:

> Meetings are a waste of time. You just find out how much the officers are paid for doing nothing. I know a couple of times I had things to bring up at

the local meeting. I went there, and it got to be 10:30 before they got over the business, reading the minutes and all the bills, and by then they said they were going to adjourn and we should come back next time. I wasted a whole evening and got nothing done. Who wants to go for a whole Saturday night and not have a chance to say anything?

Yet to an important few the meetings are rewarding ceremonies.

How many members do attend—and who are these? These questions will be taken up in the next section.

Who Attends Meetings

As has been explained, attendance at meetings observed was usually low. Table 5 gives the median, or "normal," attendance, for meetings held when no extraordinary events were scheduled. As will be seen, attendance at a vast majority of the meetings in the nineteen locals observed seemed to fluctuate around a "normal" figure, even though the figure varied from local to local.

Although the membership in these locals ranges from 110 to 4000, normal attendance varies only from 12 to 100 members. Except for skilled locals in

Table 5 / Attendance at Meetings in Locals Studied

| | | Normal Attendance | |
| | | Number | Per Cent of Membership |
Industry	Size of Local	Number	Per Cent of Membership
Manufacturing	4,000	30	1
Manufacturing	2,000	40	2
Steel	1,900	48	3
Utility (Production local)	1,800	100	6
Automobile Assembly Plant	1,800	35	2
Needle Trades (Italian local)	1,800	35	2
Needle Trades (Operators local)	1,500	75	5
Automobile Assembly Plant	1,100	70	6
Steel	900	35	4
Public Utility (White collar)	850	40	5
Manufacturing	600	20	3
Foundry	600	30	5
Needle Trades (Pressers)	600	90	15
Needle Trades (Unskilled operators)	400	25	6
Needle Trades (Cutters)	400	80	20
Needle Trades (Skilled operators)	200	60	30
Insurance Workers	150	50	33
Clerical Workers	110	12	11
Public Utility (Engineers' local)	110	26	24

the needle trades and very small locals of less than 200, attendance varies from 2 to 6 per cent.[2] In very large locals, this may drop to 1 per cent. On the other hand, proportional attendance was somewhat higher in the very small locals. This is perhaps the result of two factors:

1. In smaller meetings the average member has a greater chance to hear what is happening and to speak his piece. One local of 1,800 had an average attendance of 100, another of 110 had an attendance of 25. Yet in both locals about twenty people would speak during the meeting. One might hypothesize that attendance at meetings depends in part on one's opportunity to get the floor.

2. In one sense, the meetings of small locals are but extensions of the social life that exists in the plant. In a small local, a man may know everyone who attends, because he knows everyone in the plant. But in a larger

Table 6 / Attendance at Meetings of a Newly Organized Local of 1,800 Utility Workers

Month	No. in Attendance	Percentage of Membership	Significant Business
July	350	20	Election of temporary officers
Aug.	320	18	Discussion of contract demands and proposed seniority rules
Sept.	220	12	Nominations of permanent officers; discussion of contract questions
	150	8	Rejection of proposal to allow voting at more than one place; report on negotiations progress
Oct.	150	8	Report on negotiations progress; strike vote
Nov.	325	18	Report on completed contract
Dec.	750	42	Ratification contract
	75	4	Selection of committee to draw up constitution
Jan.	90	5	Selection of job evaluation chairman
Feb.	80	4	Blue Cross discussion; discussion of dispute with company over contract
March	85	5	Complaints about officers
April	110	6	Discussion of President's salary
May	65	4	First reading of constitution
June	110	6	Adoption of constitution
July	65	4	Discussion of grievances
Aug.	90	5	Election of convention delegates
Sept.	180	10	Nomination of officers

[2] The three needle trades locals with relatively high attendance are exceptional. These consisted predominantly of first-generation Americans in highly skilled trades. The deep emotional involvement of their members stands in sharp contrast to the other locals studied.

local, a newcomer may be familiar with only two or three faces at the meeting.

On important occasions, such as contract negotiations and elections, attendance may be increased threefold over that at regular meetings. Table 6 shows the fluctuation of attendance in a newly organized local of 1,800 members. Attendance gradually stabilized at 6 per cent after an early peak during contract negotiations.

The hard core   Gradually attendance stabilizes, so that the average meeting contains a "hard core" of regular participants plus a small number of strange "new faces,"[3] men who come to a single meeting and then are not seen for a long time. There are many such "strange faces" during negotiations. Thus, in the utility local (Table 6), 750 attended the contract ratification meetings. Of these, probably fewer than 150 went to another meeting during the next eight months. Even at regular meetings there are a small number of "strangers"—mostly men who wish to apply "pressure" on behalf of their personal grievances or those of their own particular work group. Thus, one meeting was visited by a large delegation which protested that the job evaluation committee had not conducted sufficient interviews in their department. As soon as the matter was settled, they left en masse.

Still the bulk of the attendance consists of "old faithfuls." Some have caught the political bug. Others feel that political activity will help them in the long run economically. In any case, this group of regulars can be divided roughly into six subclasses: the leaders, the personal followers of the leaders, the department representatives, the pressure groups, the social groups, and the "isolates."

The leaders   First among the hard core are the men who can be called "local-wide leaders," men who draw their political support from throughout the local. Many of these hold elective offices, but a few are "powers behind the scenes." Others are accepted as members of a semiorganized opposition.

Personal followers of the leaders   Some men come to meetings only because they are friends of a union-wide leader. When he has a special interest in impending business, he may make an exceptional effort to round up his followers. For example, in anticipation of an attempt to strip him of some of his power, one local president brought in fifteen new faces from his own department. An observer commented:

> Bob really packed the meeting. He sure wants to win. Well, he won't. But at least he has some buddies around, so he won't be alone at the bar.

[3] Attendance at twelve months of meetings was analyzed in a well-established local. Of those who came to an average meeting, 26 per cent would never come again that year, 32 per cent would come to two or to four meetings, 18 per cent from five to eight meetings, and 24 per cent to nine or more that year.

As soon as the crucial vote had been taken about half the group streamed out and the rest remained for the wake.

Department representatives Particularly in larger locals, some members attend meetings in the role of "departmental representatives." Often they are stewards, who rarely address the meeting except on matters concerning their own departments.

The stewards consider it their function to tell the men in the shop what happened at the meeting and, to a lesser extent, to tell the meeting what the men in the shop want. One leader explained her lack of concern over low attendance in these terms:

> The members hear about what happens through their steward or whoever else attends meetings. There is almost always someone from each department who does attend.

However, this situation is far from universal. In some locals, stewards are just as irregular in their attendance as the average member. Many departmental groups go unrepresented at meetings.

Pressure groups As discussed in Chapter 4, some members attend just for the purpose of putting "pressure" on the officers to consider their grievance favorably. Few members of such groups hold union office, and many are unsympathetic to the current leadership of the local. Many are fearful that the union may threaten their welfare. For instance, in one meeting men from a department waved a petition with a substantial number of signatures and shouted:

> We are sick and tired of waiting for something to be done. We want the union to do something now, not six months from now.

Social groups Another kind of group was more social. Its members looked upon the meeting primarily as a place to get together and were characterized by apparent high social solidarity, entering and leaving the union hall as a clique. Their interest in union politics was usually low. They would rarely speak on the floor and frequently would leave the meeting early. They relished "the fireworks" but soon wearied of the more prolonged arguments.

Isolates The final group observed was the "isolates." Many aspired to union leadership but somehow lacked the human relations skills required. Practically every local has its quota, and these best may be described by examples:

> Vincent O'Malley is an orator of the old school. He gets up at least once a meeting and delivers a long and windy ten, or fifteen minute speech. The

only trouble is that it rarely has anything to do with the matter at issue. He is of such a self-important and quarrelsome disposition that no one will sit with him even though he seems very anxious to make friends.

George Philbert is a tense, excitable expert on parliamentary law; he specializes in tying up union meetings in a mass of procedural red tape which constantly exasperates the chairman.

Frank Canteala is known as a "Communist." As far as can be seen, his only ideological line is sheer opposition: he is against everything and frequently asks intelligent but extremely embarrassing questions. And as a symbol of his opposition, he votes "no" on routine matters such as accepting the secretary's report.

At times, these men provide comic relief and excitement—more often their antics are merely tedious and time consuming.

The Functions of the Meeting

To the outside observer, union meetings are boring. To the average member, they may be frustrating, time-wasting experiences. Yet, to an important few, meetings are rewarding occasions. Why do some attend so faithfully, in spite of storms, fatigue, and family obligations while others are unmoved by ceaseless prodding?

The union meeting serves (1) as a ceremony, (2) as an opportunity for catharsis or bringing dissatisfactions to the attention of officers, (3) as a means for the officers to communicate with the rank and file, and (4) as an opportunity for decision-making.

Ceremony   A union is a democratic fraternal organization, a means by which the members unite for common purposes. From one point of view the meeting *is* the union. In theory, at least, the membership is supreme: all power derives from "the body" and the "body" expresses itself only in meetings. It is the only occasion that officers and members regularly meet outside of a management-dominated environment. From this point of view, the meeting is the union's most important single activity, and members often measure loyalty in terms of meeting-attendance.

In a majority of the locals studied, the members "dressed up" and wore their best clothes, indicating that this was an important ceremony. The officers, too, showed great respect for the "body."

Both leaders and members seemed to enjoy many of the ceremonies connected with the meeting, at least when they were conducted properly. Traditions such as saluting the flag, having a sergeant-at-arms pass on all who wish to enter the meeting, and escorting the International officers to the platform, had great emotional appeal. They added drama and were symbolic of the unity and common purpose of the local.

Upward communications   From one point of view, the meeting provides an opportunity for the rank-and-file members to bring their desires and needs to the attention of the union officers. Yet few meetings observed did this effectively.

Members often come to the meeting with individual grievances which they wish to discuss. Officers think the meeting time should be reserved for ratifying decisions made by the executive board and for approving progress made in bargaining. Grievances, they feel, should be left to the grievance procedure. (Of course, many members agree with them—being interested in their own grievances, but not those of others.)

Thus, there may be a covert struggle between the leaders and individual members. The officers at times try to keep the members from bringing their grievances to the floor. The rank and file persist in bringing them up. Although individual members are usually successful in being heard, they are often "out of order" from a strictly parliamentary point of view. This makes for a disorderly meeting.

Where the members cannot express their "gripes" directly, they do so indirectly. Frequently they unburden themselves by venting hostility against the officers. Their animosity and aggression are often expressed in discussions of "business matters." At times, the members are "agin" everything. A common way of showing their resentment is to attack the financial report—in particular, lost-time allowances.

When "important" issues are at stake and attendance is high, this blockage is bound to increase. Many people have something to say, yet are somehow unable to channel their remarks into the proper parliamentary "pigeonhole." The result is general frustration. When this happens, members promise themselves "That's the last time I attend one of those damn things."

Because of this, many members grow convinced that their contributions will be "out of place," or that they will be called out of order by the officers. The majority of members are bashful, fearful of speaking in public. A member confided:

> Usually a guy with a beef is afraid to get up before the meeting and talk about it, without getting a few drinks to bolster himself. Then, after they do that they don't make sense and they drag it out.

Thus union meetings are utilized as open forums for registering dissatisfactions less often than might be expected. Doubtless, many members have lost interest in attending meetings just because they do not provide satisfactory opportunities for placing grievances before the officers.

Communication downward   From the point of view of the union leaders we interviewed, the most important function of these meetings is that of downward communication. They see the meeting as a chance (1) to transmit essential information and instructions to members, (2) to activate them to support union policies, and (3) to show off results.

The union has its own system of communication, such as posting notices on the bulletin boards and passing information through the chief stewards and stewards. Still, the meeting is an important supplementary means of getting the "word" to the rank and file. For example, at one meeting routine instructions were given as follows:

> . . . so until we settle this with management, we all should refuse to accept our vacation dates.
>
> If anyone still has not turned in his raffle ticket, will he return it to me [the Treasurer] at the end of the meeting.
>
> At last, management has agreed to make available forms so that you can apply for your pension fund. You can get them from Miss Smathers in Personnel.

Particularly during negotiations or serious crises in relations with management, the officers use meetings as a means of encouraging support and building up morale. At the time of negotiations, leaders would make statements such as these:

> We need a strike vote because you can't go into negotiations with your hands tied behind your back.
>
> You can bet management is going to try to divide us. Now is the time when our local is being tested and we must stick together.

Finally, meetings are a place at which leaders can show off to the members and brag to them about the progress made.

> We really are a union now. We are showing management how strong we are.

The officers expect that the members will accept this information in a passive manner. It rarely works out that way. The information-giving period frequently develops into a question-and-answer period, and the questions asked develop into declarations of grievances. These grievances are for the most part directed against management and, to some extent, against the union for not having pushed management harder.

Time and time again a routine motion will be debated at length (with much discussion off the point), in the end winning unanimous consent. Such was the case with an executive board recommendation that it begin talks with management about progress on its job evaluation program. Everyone agreed that this was a good idea, but before it could be approved more than an hour passed while the members lambasted management for its arrogance and the union leaders for their timidity.

The union leaders feel that giving information and dispelling false rumors is the primary function of the meeting. Many of the members agree with this. When asked why they attend, they say, "I want to find out what's happening." And those who fail to show up comment, "Now that I'm going to meetings I don't know what is going on." Thus, in spite of the fact that at times the leaders are sharply questioned, perhaps the majority of the questioners are honestly seeking information.

Decision-making In theory, decision-making is the meeting's most important function, for in doing this it acts as the supreme legislative body of the local. Actually, however, except in small and new locals, few of the significant decisions are made on the union floor. In large locals, the meeting cannot perform this function effectively unless the alternatives are clearly defined.[4]

Meetings do provide opportunities for officers to communicate downward about decisions already made and for the members to communicate their fears and desires upward. Only rarely do meetings do more than ratify (or occasionally, reject) proposals brought to them by the executive committee.

Small locals are an exception. Here, membership meetings do make decisions. One local of about one hundred was observed for a period of a year, during which meeting attendance averaged twenty-five. The subject matter considered in these meetings was much like that considered in executive committees of larger locals. Intimate problems of collective-bargaining strategy were discussed in full, in a manner which contrasted sharply with that of larger locals.

Many new locals, in the first flush of enthusiasm over being able to handle their own affairs, try to make similar decisions in meetings. But unless the alternatives to be considered are somehow channeled and structured, chaos ensues. The meeting is usually unable to reach a decision and merely flounders until somebody moves to refer the matter to the executive committee or a special committee.

Gradually, in all the large locals observed, decision-making at meetings (as opposed to mere formal ratification of executive board action) was narrowed down to a relatively few functions. These included the following:

1. *Ratification of the collective bargaining contract and major supplemental agreements with management* In some locals, new job evaluation and wage incentive plans were submitted to the meeting; in others, only to the department involved. Most small, day-to-day agreements were not submitted for ratification and often not even reported to the meeting.

2. *Disposition of appeals from the grievance procedure* In every local studied, members who were dissatisfied with the disposition of their griev-

---

[4] Large meetings do make effective decisions when there is a well-organized party system. The function of parties is to sharpen and clarify the issues. However, stable party structure within the local is comparatively rare.

ances had the theoretical right to appeal to the meeting floor. Only in rare instances were individuals observed to avail themselves of this right.

Usually when these cases were referred to the "body" it was because they were "too hot" for the officer to handle. In some cases, any decision would have adversely affected a large group of members. In others the officers felt that this was the only way to "squelch a troublemaker" who was constantly annoying them by repeatedly demanding another hearing.

3. *Approval of extraordinary expense* (*chiefly for officers*)

4. *Approval of constitutional changes*

5. *Elections*   Regular elections for union-wide officers were usually held apart from the meeting. Committee appointments were normally made by the president and automatically ratified by the "body." However, in the case of the election of convention delegates and executive board members, there was often a spirited contest.

6. *Action on incidental matters brought up by the members themselves* These included contributions to charitable organizations, political resolutions, and a small number of other items which rarely took up much time.

The amount of decision-making which took place at the meetings actually varied sharply among the locals studied. In a majority there was little—if one defines decision-making as voting "yes" or "no." Instead of using a ballot, the members have learned to influence union policy by expressing their opinions at meetings and even—through silence—just by attending and letting their "weight" be felt. Much of the discussion which revolved around officers' reports and individual grievances was irrelevant in the strict parliamentary sense. Still, the officers took these members' viewpoints into account in the weeks that followed.

Actually the officers face a dilemma in deciding how many problems should be submitted to the local. Most of them strongly believe in the democratic ethic. Furthermore, it is often convenient to "pass the buck" to the "body" on hot issues. On the other hand, as we have seen, the meetings are really not suited to decision-making on difficult, technical questions.

The leadership faces a difficult problem if it follows the views of the small meeting-attending minority. The views of the active group are not always the same as those of the rank and file. In following the wishes of the "activists," the leadership may antagonize the bulk of its silent followers.

On the other hand, the officers have no sure way of knowing what the rank and file want except through the medium of the active members, for this group is the leadership's primary channel of communication with the rank and file. The "actives" influence the rank and file (chiefly through interpreting the leadership's activities) and at the same time bring the rank-and-file problems to the attention of the officers.

So a shrewd leader will listen carefully to the opinions expressed at meetings but will balance them with information obtained from other sources.

Conclusion

To a new man, a union meeting may be a collection of people who gather in a dingy hall, listen to endless speeches, and argue in a pointless manner about the complaints of one or two of them. But for the active, these members' complaints are more than "gripes," they are symbols of the union's strength; the people are not strangers but "buddies," and the meeting has a ceremonial meaning in some ways tantamount to a religious ritual.

Many enjoy the meeting because it has the excitement of a political contest. The unattractive surroundings and the tedious pace mean nothing to them because they enjoy the bickering and love to talk. Others who attend are less interested in social satisfactions. They feel that by attending meetings they will help themselves economically. This may entail silent pressures on the officers who "know why we are here" or the vocalization of specific complaints.

Of course, the meeting cannot satisfy both groups at once. It is impossible to handle internal political business and collective-bargaining business at the same time. So there are clashes between the two groups, and neither is completely satisfied, each group thinking that the other is engaged in irrelevancies.

The interminable committee reports and the rigid parliamentarianisms are often interpreted by the rank and file as attempts to "stall" and disguise the real issues. For them, the real business of the meeting is the chance to obtain redress of grievances and the opportunity to "get something off their chests."

If they are insistent enough, rank-and-file members can bring collective-bargaining matters to the attention of their officers. Although the officers may object that grievances are being brought up at the wrong time, they are still sensitive to what is said. Inefficient and boring as it may be, the meeting does serve its purpose. If a member is sufficiently interested he can have his say, and he may directly influence union policy. It should be emphasized that decisions are rarely made on the initiative of the rank and file. In fact, union meetings might well be compared with those of the British House of Commons, where the administration answers questions and defends itself, and the opposition attacks.

"Democracy" is a value-loaded word and has not been used in the discussion so far. But if by democracy one means the responsiveness of the officers to the pressures of the rank and file, an opportunity for individuals to express themselves, and a chance to decide basic issues by a majority vote, then the union meeting, for all its faults, is a democratic assemblage. In fact, except for the New England town meeting, it is almost unique in permitting participation by ordinary citizens in discussions which vitally affect their lives.

In subsequent chapters, we shall see that all groups and members do not take equal advantage of their opportunity to participate in this and other forms of union activity.

11

Patterns of Participation

An earlier chapter has described various forms of pressure which the members may exert on the officers. One of the more effective types is direct participation in the internal affairs of the local.

By *participation* we mean expenditure of time on union affairs. Participation is more than emotional involvement in unionism: it is *doing*—attending meetings, voting, running for office, paying dues, reading union newspapers, filing grievances, going on strike, bringing the family to picnics. By nominating candidates for office, voting in elections, and, of course, attending meetings, groups of members can increase the sensitivity of the leadership to their problems. However, different criteria must be used in different situations. Voting in elections, for instance, is a more sensitive index when the members must make a special trip to the union office than when the voting booth is set up outside the plant gates. Attendance at union meetings also is significant, although at times it may reflect the distance members live from the meeting hall or the shifts on which they work.

Over-all participation in union activities in the locals studied was low. Frequently less than 5 per cent of the total membership attended meetings, and it was difficult to draft men to accept minor union positions such as shop stewardships or committee memberships. Most union leaders admitted frankly that apathy was a major problem.

However, participation is not uniformly low in a given local. Meetings have been observed at which 50 per cent of the attendance came from one relatively small department. Some departments have five or six candidates for steward; in others not a single person is willing to make the race.

Why are some departments more active than others? If we can explain this we will gain added insight into the nature of the participation process itself.

This chapter suggests a circular explanation: groups participate because they obtain benefits from the union, and they obtain these benefits because they participate. The crucial factors, however, are the *impetus* for initial activity and the circumstances under which this interest is transformed into continuing successful participation. Thus groups may participate *at first* for a number of reasons, but only groups obtaining some measure of economic or political success are likely to *maintain* their interest. The data show further that high-participation groups usually exhibit internal unity, have high status in the plant community, and bear a strategic importance to the flow of production. Our emphasis throughout is on groups, because in most cases members do not participate purely as individuals.

High-Participation Groups

For many groups, participation represents an act of expediency. These "practical" members are primarily concerned with their individual grievances or special interests. They see union activity as a means of protecting themselves, either from management or from competing groups within the union. Their participation is for limited purposes and for a limited time. Innumerable examples can be given of how economic dissatisfactions lead to greater union activity.

In one case, the machinists, a strong and cohesive department, became active in organizing a new union when they learned that a similar group in another plant of the same company was receiving higher earnings. They had hopes that the new union would eliminate this differential. In another case, wheelroom men believed that technological change was restricting their job opportunities. They felt that the union could win for them a wider promotional ladder. A group of binders protested to their supervisor that relatives of high company officials were obtaining promotions more rapidly than the rest of the men. When the supervisor's answer was unsatisfactory, they began to attend union meetings. In some of these cases, initial interests led to continuing participation; in others it did not. An example of each outcome is presented below:

The framefitters tired of union activity when their grievances were not attended to. On the other hand, the relayers found that union participation brought unexpected success and they developed a lasting interest.

The Case of the Framefitters

The framefitters were very active in organizing the union. They hoped that it would be successful in eliminating subcontractors (maintenance men from other companies doing work within the plant under contract) and that, as a result, there would be promotions for everyone.

The officers of the new union negotiated with management for over a year without making significant progress. During this time the members became increasingly dissatisfied with the way things were going. Initially, there was no decline in their attendance at local meetings. The first indication of discontent was an increase in sniping at the officers at departmental meetings. When this failed to speed up negotiations, more drastic action was suggested. The following conversation took place between a framefitter and a union officer:

> Fitter: What we ought to do is get rid of the no-strike clause. I'm not sure whether you have the guts to do that—but that's what we have to do. If we could go out on strike, we could show the company what we meant.
>
> Officer: I sympathize with you entirely. But that's not the way to approach the problem. You're going to wait till the contract expires—and then, if necessary, we will go on strike.
>
> Fitter: Sure, that's the way it always is. You guys always talk strike, but you never do anything about it.

An increasingly common observation among this group was, "That's the way it always happens. Those boys sell out." Along with this loss of faith in the union, the framefitters' attendance at departmental and local meetings began to decline. Members remarked, "What's the point of listening to them make excuses?" Thus, the framefitters lost their interest in unionism when they couldn't get action.

The Case of the Relayers

The experience of the relayers with unionism was much more favorable even though they were in a technologically declining department in which job opportunities were diminishing.

In 1939, the relayers found an exceptionally able leader in the person of "Red" Newcomb. Newcomb built them into a tightly organized political bloc and won election to the local executive committee. Through strategic manipulation of political forces he won the relayers a special 5-cents-an-hour wage increase—an increase which put them out of line with the rest of the men doing work requiring the same skill. Naturally these other men reacted violently, but the wage differential was not eliminated until 1941. By this time the relayers were convinced that political action within the union did "pay off."

As a consequence, a tradition of union activity was started. Even after the relayers lost their wage differential they remained active. Several were elected to office, and though they never again won anything so outstanding as their 5-cents-an-hour differential, they secured many other benefits.

As a result, they have remained active. Although they comprise but 5 per cent of the union's membership, they often provide 25 per cent of the meeting attendance. In 1951, they elected two of their members to an eight-man executive board. Several things happened in this case:

1. By the force of his own enthusiasm, Red Newcomb persuaded his fellow workers that they could protect their economic position through taking part in union activities. He accomplished this because he was liked and respected by the group.

2. After members of the group became active, they won political as well as economic success. Although their original motivation was economic, as they learned more about the union their interest deepened. Newcomb was no longer alone in his political ambitions; a number of other members aspired to office.

3. Finally, going to union meetings provided the relayers with the same kinds of social satisfactions as bowling or other forms of after-hours activity. Union politics provided the subject matter for conversation at work. The group made the union its cause.

The relayers' story is far from unique. Many individuals or groups participate at first for limited "practical" purposes only. And then, as they go to more and more meetings, they catch the union fever and continue their activity even after their immediate objectives have been achieved.

Non- or Low-Participation Groups

First, it should be emphasized that we found little correlation between union activity and expressed dissatisfaction with working conditions. It is true that highly active groups are frequently outspoken in their complaints, but so are those which are completely inactive!

Numerous examples can be given where the degree of the workers' dissatisfaction seemed to have little to do with the extent of their union participation. Take the case of two adjacent shops in a large mill, each putting out the same product and each being paid according to the same piecework system. In one shop, the equipment was modern, while in the other it was forty years old. The workers in the second shop had to put forth twice as much effort as the first to obtain equivalent earnings. Nevertheless, participation in both groups was almost identically low.

Some inactive groups have tried participation without success; others, as far as can be discovered, have never made the attempt. Yet, in both types of groups there seems to be something that could be described as a feeling of "minority status"—the union is really for others, "our small bunch just doesn't have a chance."

In part, this attitude is an intensification of general rank-and-file lethargy: "Let the actives run the union." In addition, there is a strong sentiment that the cards are stacked, that "there is no use in even trying to get the union to see our point of view." For example, the barrel cleaners in a chemical plant also were resigned: "This is the dirtiest job in the plant and the union never gets back here."

This is a common attitude among women in predominantly male locals:

> There is no use asking for an increase (in pay); some of the fellows in the union think we're making too much money already doing this work and certainly shouldn't get more.

Among high-skilled groups which have been unsuccessful in their attempts to dominate the union this attitude can also be prevalent. The following are comments from one such low-participating group:

> We really ought to have a union of our own. We'd have done a lot better than we have now.
>
> It's my opinion that if it wasn't for the union, rather than $2.50 an hour, we'd be getting $3.50. You know this union has got one thing in mind—and that is to bring the lower paid workers up to the higher paid. They don't really recognize the craftsmen. They want to pay everyone almost the same.

Some groups lose their battles almost by default. Being convinced that participation is useless, they act accordingly. In a department which had been split by an internal battle of serious proportions over scheduling, an informed observer said:

> The men on the second and third tricks could outvote us on this thing any time they wanted to. The trouble is, they don't come to meetings. They figure that since they're the first ones to be booted out of a plant, if there is a layoff, they shouldn't really have much interest in these things.

Such a defeatist attitude toward participation further reduces the group's bargaining position. The circular process continues: lower participation results in less attention being paid to their economic demands—this, in turn, intensifies their disinclination to take part in union activity.

All this, then, provides additional evidence that groups will participate only if they feel the union offers economic, political, or social satisfactions.

Four Patterns of Group Participation

This still leaves unanswered why some groups are more likely to obtain success from union activity than others.

A recent field work suggests that there exist consistent and predictable differences in the manner in which work groups relate to management and the union. The four rather distinct types of groups observed were characterized as erratic, strategic, conservative, and apathetic.[3]

Erratic Groups

In the Erratic groups there was no apparent relationship between how seriously members felt their grievances and the intensity of their protests. Minor issues that might have been easily settled often developed into major uprisings (such as unforeseen wildcat strikes). At the same time, many deep-seated grievances festered over long periods with no apparent group reaction. Union leaders found this "split personality" hard to understand. Petty grievances often escalated into nearly insolvable problems because of rash demonstrations, while important cases languished in the grievance procedure because there was no support from the rank and file for efforts of union officers to convince management that "this is really important to the men."

From management's point of view, these groups were dangerously explosive. Both management and union officials devoted much time and energy to these tension areas. Even so, they often admitted frankly "you just don't know what to expect," in such departments.

Sometimes the atmosphere of this kind of group suddenly changes a department that had been a source of endless grief to all concerned to one of the showplaces of the plant, where unanimity and harmony prevail. And then, later on, it may just as suddenly revert to its earlier condition.

Strategic Groups

In many plants, one or two groups were the focus of most of the really important economic grievances. These groups often participated actively in union affairs as a means of pressuring union officers to advance the groups' specific economic interests. Time after time, members of these groups succeeded in electing one of their number to top union office, even when they comprised only a small fraction of the membership. These departments were not characterized by sudden flashes of activity; rather, they were shrewdly calculating pressure groups that never tired of objecting to unfavorable management decisions, of seeking loopholes in existing policies and contract clauses that would be to their benefit, and of comparing their benefits with those of other departments in the plant. They demanded constant attention for their problems and reinforced their demands by group action.

Unlike the Erratic groups, however, the amount and kind of pressure the

[3] Most of the remainder of this chapter is based on Leonard Sayles, *Behavior of Industrial Work Groups; Prediction and Control* (New York: Wiley, 1958).

Strategic groups exerted was carefully measured, both against the objectives they sought and the immediate strategy of the total situation. Thus, management was startled with a sudden display of aggression only if surprise was chosen from the many weapons at their disposal. Like actors they could "turn it on or off" ("it" being such concerted activities as slowing down work) as the occasion demanded. To that degree, their behavior was predictable.

Such groups are often at the heart of the union as well as of the grievance activities in their plants. The way management handles the difficult problems that arise in such departments is a prime factor in determining the existing climate of industrial relations.

Conservative Groups

Of the groups observed, the Conservative groups were the most stable, in that they were least likely to take concerted action without warning. Their compensation and working conditions were so satisfactory that it was commoner for management to have more grievances against them than they had against management; for example, it was not unusual for the company to initiate negotiations with the group in order to obtain a higher output.

Conservative groups pushed few grievances. On the surface, at least, they showed little evidence of turmoil, trouble, or concerted activity. At times they exercised strength, but, once proven, their strength, like that of any great power, was accepted at face value by those whom it affected.

Being fully aware of their strength, such groups do not demand the immediate service often insisted upon by other groups. They accept the time-consuming routine and red tape of the grievance procedure without exploding from frustration. (When made to wait, weaker groups are more likely to fear they will lose their grievance unless they do something, and quickly.)

Representatives from these Conservative groups might be termed the senior statesmen of the plant negotiation machinery. Pyrotechnics are usually out of place for them, although when occasion warrants, a quick stoppage is always a possibility. As the elite of the plant labor force, they are self-assured, successful, and relatively stable in their relations with management and in the internal affairs of their group.

On occasion, they exhibit ambivalence toward the union. They may experiment with leadership and then leave active affairs indefinitely. They may even withdraw from the unified bargaining unit in favor of some craft union that will better represent them.

Apathetic Groups

By almost any measure, the Apathetic departments were the least likely to develop grievances or engage in concerted action as a means of pressuring management or the union. Although occasional incidents did occur, compared with other groups, these workers were not inclined to challenge decisions or attempt to gain something extra for themselves. Surprisingly, however, these departments were not ranked highest by management for consistent productivity and cooperativeness.

These groups were also less prone to engage in union politics or participate in the internal life of their unions. Petty jealousies and interpersonal problems were somewhat more common than in the other groups and cohesion was less strong. Although management and union representatives could identify certain influential members of the group, real leadership was dispersed among a relatively large number of individuals.

Factors Determining Character of Groups

The behavior differences described above are not randomly distributed. Regardless of the plant in which they are located, the quality of supervision, or the expressed policies of union or management, certain kinds of work groups are strategic groups. The behavior of others, again with identifiable differences, is nearly always described as erratic. What are the factors determining the type of group that will develop?

On the basis of the organization chart, work flow, and layout of an industrial plant, specific predictions regarding work group behavior can be made confidently. Jobs with certain characteristics will probably be centers of industrial-relations problems; jobs with other characteristics are unlikely to embody such frictions.

Technology

It appears that the most relevant variable is the *technological system* used by the company to organize the work process. The independence or dependence among workers in the flow of work, the number and similarity of jobs in any one location, and the indispensability of any part with respect to the whole are largely determined by plant layout, the kinds and quantity of equipment, and the skills required by the job.

Industrial relations problems are common to jobs which are unpleasant, repetitive, mechanically paced, heavy, dirty, or exacting in terms of the quantity and quality of output required. However, group structure as determined by the technological process may also create industrial-relations problems.

Common Interests

Employees who work physically close to each other but operate different kinds of machines or perform different tasks have little in common. They rarely combine for common objectives and so frequently form apathetic groups.

What seems essential for uniting people to act together might be called *resonance*. Resonance results when people have identical experiences, so that each person can hear his own grievances shared, repeated, and magnified. With sympathetic repetition, the problem grows in importance. A group of like-minded employees may convince one another not only that something *should* be done but, more important, that it *can* be done. Other things being equal, the greater the number of workers affected by some aspect of the work environment, the greater the likelihood that they will act in concert.

What distinguishes the Erratic from the Strategic group if both are highly resonant? To answer this it is necessary to look more closely at groups in which interdependence among employees is imposed by technology.

Independent homogeneous crews   These work groups are usually composed of three to twelve employees who work together at identical jobs, but independently. Crews loading or unloading materials or sanding automobile bodies are examples of homogeneous crews. Resonance is at a maximum because the work throws them together. But the behavior of this type of group is Erratic, not Strategic. Why?

Part of the explanation may be found in the intimacy of their relationship. Because they are so close to each other, slight problems are quickly magnified. Communication is fast and reinforced by the group's completely shared experiences. Thus, a really embittered employee or a highly satisfied worker with leadership potential can have startling effects on the attitudes and behavior of the other workers. Such work groups are incapable of long, carefully planned attacks on management or union decisions they dislike. They react immediately and often unwisely. Their inability to restrain themselves makes carefully calculated pressure activities unlikely.

Homogeneous crews have another handicap. Because of the close, almost family-like relationships they foster, it is difficult for them to ally themselves with the larger, more inclusive, department units, an alliance which is necessary in order to process important problems through union channels.

Interdependent crews and short assembly lines   Work crews and short assembly lines in which each employee has a different job need internal unity more than does an aggregation of employees who work independently. The technologically interdependent workers must come to a mutually acceptable decision concerning the pace of work and total output. Although the high frequency of their interaction makes them a tightly knit work team, the conflicting needs of the several occupations included in the group (with different job classifications and skills) can prevent the crew from working together as a whole. Consequently, work crews and short assembly lines do not engage in prolonged, carefully planned concerted activity on their own behalf. They are either Apathetic or, in a few cases, Erratic.

Furthermore, since these groups are not free to select and change their informal leadership, the functional work leader selected for them (the straw boss or crew chief) usually dominates the situation. More tolerant of (or more accustomed to) highly dominant, inflexible leadership, they allow their own leaders to act as straw bosses and, in many situations, to fill in as first-line supervisors during the temporary absences of foremen, a dual responsibility that normally would not be permitted in groups of technologically independent workers.

These groups frequently engage in spontaneous demonstrations such as wildcat strikes. When frustrations build up in a group with no systematic means of expressing its discontent its members may appear to be relatively satisfied for a long period—suddenly an explosion occurs.

Long assembly lines Longer assembly lines, on which workers are restricted in their interaction with workers on either side of them, tend to develop weak informal groups.

A study of an assembly line consisting of thirty-five workers found that conditions encouraged the formation of tightly knit pairs of workers while other operators became socially isolated. The workers in the study were stationed at a moving belt doing simple wiring and soldering operations.

> An operator could talk easily only with workers on her immediate right and left. From the point of view of any one worker, her only possible spontaneous group during working hours consisted of two workers and herself, or a group of three. A threesome, however, tends to make a very unstable group because of the likelihood of pairing. It is easy, therefore, for some operators at least to find themselves socially isolated. Once something goes wrong, there is considerable interaction, but under conditions of extreme tension and anxiety.[4]

This kind of behavior is typical of the Apathetic groups observed by the authors.

Work-Flow Breaks and Imperfections

Many Erratic groups were located at points in an assembly or material flow situation where communication was difficult. Often two or more sections needed to coordinate their actions to avoid breakdowns and other mishaps (many of which could hurt production, result in lost incentive earnings or necessitate additional physical labor). However, because of the plant layout,

---

[4] A. Zaleznik, *Worker Satisfaction and Development* (Cambridge, Mass.: Harvard Business School, Division of Research, 1956), pp. 120–121.

physical or temporal separations kept the groups apart, making adequate communication impossible. This resulted in production difficulties that erupted into employee-management fireworks.

Time and again communications problems led to lower production and then to lower piece-work earnings. As a consequence, employees became resentful and frequently focused their discontent on the work standards. Their resentment led to grievances and further diminished output. Management reacted by placing pressure on both workers and supervisory personnel to raise their output levels, and this led to further lowering of morale and output. Thus, a modest technical problem can create a sharp, downward-spiraling productivity curve.

Indispensability

Work groups in a position to halt production used this economic power to get material gains for themselves. These groups are often of the Strategic type.

One study found striking differences between the wildcat strike records of companies in the rubber tire industry and those of firms manufacturing electrical goods.[5] Technologically, these two industries are at opposite poles. Many individual groups, by taking concerted action in a tire plant, can throw thousands out of work. This interruption of routine creates a strong backlash, because groups that do not have the original grievance still suffer the stress of work interruptions. On the other hand, there is little fixed sequence of operations in the manufacture of electrical goods; it is easy to "work around" a blockage caused by one group's strike or slowdown. The greater leverage enjoyed by tire plant workers increases the likelihood that management will yield to concerted action. Less immediate results in electrical-manufacturing plants discourage the use of self-help measures.

Thus, individual work groups have enormous leverage in companies that follow traditional functional patterns of organization and where a stoppage in one department has immediate and drastic repercussions in adjacent departments. Minor frictions, causing modest interruptions in the work pace, snowball to major proportions. Employees quickly learn the lesson that a small number of them can put pressure on management many times greater than their size would suggest.

Status of the Job

For the most part, Strategic groups occupied jobs that were near the top, but not at the top, of the plant's status ladder. Often there were elements of

[5] James Kuhn, *Bargaining in Grievance Settlement* (New York: Columbia University Press, 1961).

ambiguity (status inconsistencies) about their prestige level. In some respects, according to their own reckoning, they were as good as those at the top. They thought that their work required as much skill and training and offered as much difficulty as that of the highest paid employees. But there was always a fatal flaw, somehow management and the world had conspired to give them something less than they deserved:

Welders are a good example. In whatever plant we went, these craftsmen, who usually received rates of pay below those of skilled occupations like electrician, saw themselves as underpaid and overworked. They were the spearhead of countless grievances to better their relative position. In most places, one needed only to mention welders to management to cause them to wince: "Those guys are hardly more skilled than a machine operator, but they think they are regular journeymen."

Other examples of work groups that are almost, but not quite at the top of the skill and status ladders of their respective organizations are centerless grinders who are almost machinists, technicians who are almost engineers, metal finishers who are almost craftsmen, and the trimmers on auto assembly lines who work with fabrics rather than metal and consider themselves the equivalent of craftsmen.

Many groups that could be classified Conservative were made up of top-status employees, often maintenance workers. At the other extreme, there was a heavy proportion of low-status laboring, machine-tending, and packaging employees represented in Apathetic groups.

Thus it appears that, for the most part, workers with higher status are more likely to participate in union affairs than those with low status. If this at first seems startling, it should be recalled that men from lower-paid jobs are generally younger or considered less competent. As a consequence, when they participate they may be thought of as upstarts; their contributions are sometimes pointedly ignored. Consequently, these men soon lose their desire to take part. It is not difficult to discourage participation.

High pay is not the only factor determining the worker's prestige. Age, sex, ethnic factors, seniority, job skill, position on the production line, value of material handled, and a host of other influences enter into the evaluation of a worker's status. All these affect the respect paid a worker by his fellows and consequently determine whether his participation is encouraged or discouraged.[7]

It is not difficult to assess the relative status of various departments or groups in a plant. People soon tell you, "They're the group that really counts around here"; "Over in our department, it is pretty much up to the day shift; everyone looks to us to start things"; "Those young guys haven't been here long enough to know what they want."

---

[7] These same factors contribute to the selection of union officers.

The following cases may give some indication of the complexity of the status factors involved in specific situations.

A clerical department   A department in a clerical local was divided into three sections—A, B, and C—each containing about twenty workers. All worked in a single large office. There were a few men in Section C; the rest were women. The type of work, the pay, and the percentage voting in a recent election were as follows:

Section	Type of Work	Pay[8]	Percent Voting
A	Making routine notations on cards	$41.00	29
B	Writing on cards (many special cases; making phone calls outside department	$41.00	61
C	Wide variety of jobs, none requiring individual discretion	$50.72	72

[8] These and other wages cited in this chapter reflect pay levels in 1950.

The line of progression, which was determined by seniority, ran from Section A, to B, to C. Sections A and B received the same pay, but the amount of responsibility and the seniority of the girls in Section B was higher. Apparently, this added status resulted in higher participation. As can be seen, participation followed strictly the seniority line.

Seven needle trades locals   Four needle trades locals had high participation; three had low. Attendance in the high-participation locals ranged from 15 to 25 per cent at routine meetings to 70 to 90 per cent at important ones. Two of these high-participation locals were made up of cutters and pressers, whose high-paid jobs were held almost entirely by men and were traditionally the keystones of the trade. The other two were small locals, representatives of declining trades (their markets having shifted to cheaper products). They were comprised almost entirely of older workers, immigrant Jews who could speak English only with difficulty.

The three low-participation locals were much larger and consisted primarily of semiskilled workers. They included two operators' locals and an Italian local. Attendance at all meetings varied from 1 to 20 per cent.

Within these low-participation locals only a small segment was active. In one operators' local, this active group came largely from workers in "quality" shops. This group had a much higher proportion of male workers than the rest of the local. In the Italian local, participation came largely from the pressers, a high-paid job always filled by men. In the last of these three locals, however, union activity could be attributed more to outside political interest. A vocal leftist minority provided the bulk of the leadership and participation.

In all the locals, the least active were the "miscellaneous trades" or the "minority crafts"—low-paid, day-rated jobs requiring less skill than the machine operations. The members were agreed that "the minority crafts just don't attend meetings."

Summarizing, participation in these needle trades locals was a function of (1) the pay and prestige of the job, (2) sex, (3) ethnic factors, and (4) political ideology.

A machine shop An isolated machine-shop department had few contacts with the rest of the plant and was sharply divided along job class lines as follows:

Job Class	Average Earnings	Number in Group
Laborers	$52	75
Helpers	$55	43
Mechanics I & II	$65–75	36

Prior to 1945, promotions with this department were extremely rare. A man hired as a laborer or as a helper would normally spend the rest of his life in that job. It took a wartime sit-down strike to establish the principle of promotion from within. More recently, a new man could start as a laborer and work his way up to Mechanic I. The first members of this new postwar crew are now reaching the top of the helper group and will soon become mechanics.

Before the war there were sharp class differences between the mechanics, helpers, and laborers. Today the division between mechanics and helper has somewhat lessened, but the division between laborers and the others continues.

The prewar laborers had little education and spoke English poorly. Of this group, thirty-three remain. Nine are broken-accented Irish, twenty-two first-generation Italians. None is considered eligible for promotion to helper or mechanic. In spite of the fact that all forty-two postwar laborers have been picked for eventual promotion to mechanic and are high-school graduates, the laborer retains the reputation of being uneducated and different. Particularly among the older-service mechanics there is little recognition that the composition of the laborer group is changing. As a consequence, there is little communication between the two groups. Mechanics will tell you:

> The laborers stick to themselves—most of them don't speak English.
> It's funny how you hang your hat and coat together, work together, yet hardly ever talk to the laborer.

Participation by laborers, particularly by the prewar group, has been low. This is true both at departmental and at union-wide meetings. To our knowledge, only one laborer has ever spoken during a union-wide meeting. Although laborers comprise half the employees in a department, their attendance is far smaller than that of mechanics. Some of the older mechanics say, "They just aren't interested in meetings—they wouldn't understand what goes on."

Prior to the war the helper had almost no chance of promotion. As one postwar mechanic said:

> In those days, the helpers really got treated like dirt. The mechanic was king and the helper was his valet. The mechanic would never do any of the dirty work. Today things are different but some of the old feeling remains.

Two of the older mechanics saw the situation this way:

> Something had to be done for the helper, but I think things have gone too far. Management has had to talk to several mechanics for letting their helpers get out of hand. The helper has got to learn. There are lots of things he doesn't know even yet.
>
> Nowadays mechanics and helpers sometimes exchange work. There's hardly a line between them. For my money that makes them learn faster, but that sure is a change.

Using attendance at union-sponsored department meetings as a measure of participation, we obtained these results:

| | | Attendance at Dept. Meeting | |
Job Class	Number in Group	Average	Maximum
Laborers	75	2	8
Helpers	43	6	22
Mechanics	36	20	31

Thus, participation is concentrated in the high-status mechanics, even though the promotional ladder has now been clearly established.

A soft-drink plant   A soft-drink plant was divided into two sharply separated departments: trucking and production. Both departments were represented by a city-wide teamsters' local. The truckers earned almost twice as much as the production workers. Although one steward was nominally supposed to represent the entire department, the production workers never participated in his election. In fact, the steward said, "If they want a steward, let them elect one."

The informal leader of the production workers admitted:

> We are a gang by ourselves. We take care of ourselves. The drivers have
> nothing to do with us. We aren't in the union. All we do is pay dues. If we
> were in the union, we'd have a shop steward. That union is for drivers.

When the time came for the plant to take part in a union shop election (as
provided for by the Taft-Hartley Act in the period 1947–51), none of the
production workers took part—and the union failed, by a one-vote margin
to win the support of the legally required absentee majority of those eligible
to vote.

A production worker commented:

> Why the hell should I vote in the union's election? What have those bas-
> tards ever done for me? They don't want me, and I don't want them.

A broken-box carpenter said:

> Sure, I know all about the union. My brother-in-law is in it. He's a driver.
> He said that election wasn't for the production workers. It was for the union
> [meaning the truckers]. I figured that was right because we didn't vote in
> other elections. Nobody gives a damn for us. If you drive a truck, you're a
> big shot—but what would they do if they didn't have any boxes?

There was no question of relative participation. The production workers
totally ignored the union and assumed that the union ignored them. The
truckers, on the other hand, *were* the union.

All the cases described above include examples of how status affects participation. In most of them, the status factor involved was one of pay. However, Sections A and B in the clerical department case received the same pay.
Here the difference was apparently seniority and job responsibility. In the
needle trades, ethnic factors were important, although the left-wing issue
played its part. Helpers and laborers in the machine shop case received almost the same average pay ($55 a week, as against $52), yet their meeting
attendance was considerably different. Here status was as much determined
by subjective evaluations as by weekly pay. The laborers were considered to
be beneath the machinists and the helpers.

Nature of the Work

Some jobs leave a man so exhausted that he has no desire to take part in
union activities when his workday is over. Others afford him plenty of opportunity to discuss union affairs while on the job and also leave him fresh
to spend long hours after work.

Take, for instance, the engine overhaul crew in an antiquated plant. These
men were extremely well paid and had high status and social unity. They
stuck together during sit-downs and slow-downs. In interviews, most of them
expressed great interest in their union. Yet their attendance at membership

meetings was low—because they averaged a 55-hour work week, and, as one man said:

> When we get finished, we are too pooped to do much more than sit home, see the TV, and go to sleep.

Compare these to the route collectors in a service union. When these men had finished their assigned route their day's work was over. A good man could easily finish in six hours and many of them devoted their extra hours to union activity.

In almost every industry, there are a few occupations whose main duty is to stand by for an emergency. Of one such group it was said:

> Those guys are like firemen. They have nothing better to do than talk union.

The same holds true of groups of men who work in close proximity on semiautomatic equipment. People from both union and management have told us: "Those guys have so much time on their hands they haven't got anything to do but gripe."

Conclusion

In a particular union, groups with high participation are not necessarily those which are most dissatisfied with working conditions. Many departments with the lowest morale are also the least active. Before dissatisfaction can be translated into participation, certain other conditions must be met. One of these, of course, is the existence of respected *leaders* within the group who are interested in taking part in union activity. But this is not enough. For, if other *group factors* are uniformly unfavorable, probably no leader, however dynamic, will be able to get the department to take an active part in the union. On the other hand, if the group factors are favorable, someone usually will be able to step forward and serve as a catalyst, and around him union activity will develop.

The important thing is to distinguish between motivation for initial union activity and that for its continuance. Provided the group is fairly well united, accidental factors may encourage one of their leaders to "try out" union activity as a means of obtaining relief from unsatisfactory work conditions. By his personal drive he may galvanize the group to action and set the stage for the growth of long-run interest.

12

Women and Minority Groups

The discussion of membership participation and selection of officers has considered the effects of such factors as pay, job location, and informal organization. All these relate to the "inplant" environment. Equally
important variables are those of sex and nationality. The relationship of
women and minority ethnic groups to the union is much less determined by
what happens in the plant than by community attitudes and the cultural background of the membership.

Women

Women present a major problem to the union. Not only are they hard to
organize but, once organized, they are less likely to participate. However, the
number of female employees is growing. They are heavily concentrated in
the clerical and service industries. A few unions, particularly those in the
needle trades, have had years of experience with female membership. Others,
such as the auto- and steelworkers, have only recently entered the clerical
field.

Women were rarely elected to office in the locals observed unless they
comprised a very obvious majority of the unit in question. A local which was

80 per cent female had but five women on its 27-member executive board. In another, half of whose members were women, the entire six-man executive board was male, as were eleven of twelve chief stewards. Two of these chief stewards' constituencies were over 80 per cent female.

Perhaps a major barrier to female participation is a feeling shared by men and women alike, that union activity is strictly a man's job. Many rank-and-file male unionists show signs of resenting female "intrusion," while the women seem to agree that their place is in the home rather than in the union hall.

One president commented:

> Women in a local are a lot of trouble. They are either trying to use their charms to get you to do something for them, or people are accusing you of using your office to make time. It just doesn't pay.

That union officers find it difficult to adjust to female membership is quite understandable. Most lower-middle and lower-class associations in America are purely male or purely female. As a rule, mixed associations are found only in the upper and upper-middle classes. Therefore, it is not surprising that most of the really active women in a white-collar local come from middle-income families.

Some women feel that participation would be hopeless. In a plant that was one-third female, some of the women concluded: "It wouldn't do any good to get active anyhow. The men think we are earning too much money already."

There are other reasons why women are not active. Married women have home obligations, but even unmarried girls often have important chores around the house. And many women, particularly the unmarried, feel that they are in the labor force only temporarily. As one leader put it:

> The unmarried women never give up hope. Even if they are fifty, they always expect some Sir Launcelot to come along and carry them away. If they are active in the union they admit defeat. They can't do that.

There is also a common stereotype in our society that unions are violent, aggressive, and very masculine. It is felt that they are not the kind of organization a respectable girl joins—certainly they are not the kind of organization in which a respectable girl should want to become active.

Union meetings are essentially masculine affairs. Even though swearing is kept to a minimum when women are present, this happens often enough to make some women uncomfortable. And after several hours of discussion, meeting halls become stuffy and smoke laden. Theresa Wolfson points out:

> Usually she [the female union member] is a stickler for a modicum of cleanliness in the places she frequents, be it shop or union hall, [yet] . . .

most union halls are dirty and unattractive. The room is filled with smoke, the floors are decorated with spittoons, the windows are usually closed and the air is chokingly foul.[1]

This problem was faced by a white-collar local which met in the commercial district. Its membership of 800 was equally divided between men and women. Yet, in early meetings there was an attendance of fewer than 15 women compared to 150–160 men. The women complained that they were frightened of going home alone. They would wait for the men to escort them to the subways. Finally the union moved its meeting place to a large midtown hotel. Although attendance as a whole fell off because a union contract had been successfully negotiated, that of women increased. Within three months after the change the proportion of women attending increased from 20 to 60 per cent. Roughly this same proportion was maintained throughout the next ten months in which the local was observed.

Attempts to encourage participation   Some unions have had success in increasing interest and participation on the part of their women members. Suspecting that given both opportunity and encouragement women would play a more active role, several locals tried to increase their female attendance through greater social and educational content in their meetings.

Many officers felt that such efforts were not worth the trouble. The following comment came from an officer of one union which is well known for its education program:

> Sure, we get some of the younger girls into choral, dramatic and designing groups. But these girls don't stay in the union long. It's a waste of time and money. Sure, if we had dances Saturday night we would have a good attendance, the girls would feel warm toward the union. But they don't stay in the union.

Such things, however, are important to the female members. One girl who regularly attended meetings said:

> It's not much fun when there aren't any men. There's one fellow who shows up once in a while, and he makes it more lively. It's not just getting dates and things like that—it's just more interesting when there are men around.

One local had the custom of spending its recreational funds on an annual beer party or dance. But when women took over the recreation committee they decided to invite "a good lecturer who will give us a good educational talk."

Those unions which have interested themselves in the special problems in-

[1] Theresa Wolfson, *The Woman Worker and the Trade Unions* (New York: International Publishers, 1926), pp. 167–168.

volved in obtaining female participation have found a new source of energy for union activity.

Ethnic Factors[2]

Although the number of foreign-born workers in industry is declining, ethnic differences, even among second-generation Americans, still play an important role. Open disputes along nationality lines, with name calling and the rest, were rarely observed. Nevertheless, ethnic differences still play an important part in determining who is elected to leadership and the degree to which various groups participate.

First- and second-generation Americans belong to many associations, but few of these cut across ethnic lines. In one community which we studied, the Moose were predominantly Italian, the Knights of Columbus were Polish, and the Masons and Elks were Anglo-Saxon. For many first- and second-generation workers in this community, the union provides their first experience in inter-ethnic associations. Naturally some conflicts are inevitable.

In Union Politics

At times, ethnic differences are more clearly defined than an outsider might imagine. One local has been the scene of a seesaw battle between the Italian and the Irish members ever since it was organized. Both sides struggled for the Anglo-Saxon-Scotch vote. In commenting about their opponents, the Irish would explain, "Well, of course, he is Italiano." And the Italians were equally curt.

In other locals, the struggle was less open. For instance, one needle trades union was the scene of a long-term struggle between Jews and Italians. Although Jews comprised less than a minority of members, about 70 per cent of the officers were Jewish. But the Italians were hopeful. As one Italian shop chairman put it:

> The future is with us. The other race is beginning to feel that they're a little better. They send their children to college and into the offices. Soon we will run the union.

In most situations, ethnic differences are significant. In spite of the unions' equalitarian ideology, union leaders observed are no more free from prejudice and discrimination than is the average member of the community from which they come. Again and again it is said that such-and-such a nationality group is too lazy to take office or that the members take office "just for what they can get for themselves." Even officers who might have been inclined to a

[2] We have no direct research experience in locals with any sizable number of Negro members.

nonprejudicial attitude toward various ethnic groups found that intraunion politics often forced them to make a choice.

In two situations observed, rival ethnic groups were of equal strength. In these, the local president was elected from among the small minority of Anglo-Saxons. In each case, the president's most difficult task was to avoid charges of favoritism by one group or another. One of these situations involved Poles and Italians in a steel local, the other Jews and Italians in a needle trades local.

Differences in Participation Patterns

Not only is there a covert struggle between ethnic groups, but differences often emerge in the participation pattern of these various groups.

For most immigrant groups, all aspects of industrial life, but particularly unionism, are completely new experiences. The Welsh, Scottish and Jewish groups are significant exceptions; they brought unionism with them from overseas. It is no coincidence that Lewis, Murray, and Hillman were the founders of the C.I.O.

For the Russian Jews who came to this country at the turn of the century, unionism had an almost religious significance. Political activity, the Workman's Circle, and unionism were all tied up into one.

> The Jewish group, because of its background, had developed a view of the trade union different from that prevailing in other trades where the racial balance is different. To the radical-minded Jewish trade unionist, his union is an instrument for economic, social, and spiritual advance, and regeneration in a world which he views with fear, if not animosity. His union is his political party and church, the depository of his social hopes and dreams.[3]

First-generation Jews, who still dominate many needle trades locals, in general have a tremendous loyalty both to their union and to its leaders (a loyalty which doubtless reflects the strong bonds of Jewish family life). This loyalty is reciprocated by the mild, paternalistic attitudes of the leaders toward their followers. The pattern of control in such unions as the Clothing Workers, the Ladies' Garment Workers, and the Upholsterers has a substantially different "feel" from that of the Longshoremen or the Building Trades—even though economically these industries are in many ways similar. All have strong leadership, but as a whole the former are far more paternalistic than the latter.

Old World and New World Jewish cultural orders placed great value on intellectualism and learning. The early Jewish unionist was a great theorist.

[3] J. B. S. Hardman, "Postscripts to Ten Years of the Labor Movement," *American Labor Dynamics,* J. B. S. Hardman, Ed. (New York: Harcourt, Brace & World, 1928), p. 29.

Thus, internal struggles in Jewish unions have often had their foundation in ideological disputes.

The Socialist tradition of the Jewish immigrants, combined with their close ties to the Russian scene, may help to explain the many fights over the issue of communism in the 1920's. Jewish locals were badly split by the issue. On the other hand, Italian locals in the garment industry were hardly affected. The ideological motivation of politics in Jewish unions contrasts sharply with that in unions which are predominantly Irish or Italian. The struggles observed in an Irish-Italian local seemed to involve much more kaleidoscopic patterns of loyalty than in the Jewish unions. In part, they seem to reflect sheer love of battle, rather than external principles.

There are sharp differences in the participation patterns of different ethnic groups. In one community, Jewish attendance at membership meetings in a needle trades union was higher than the Italian. In an auto local, relative Irish participation was greater than that of Italians, while the French had the worst record of all. In a steel local, the largest ethnic group was Polish but the Italians provided a majority of the officers.

Declining Importance of Ethnic Differences

From generation to generation these ethnic differences tend to decline. Initially, for instance, there was a considerable difference in the participation pattern of Jewish and Italian women. Female Jewish immigrants were almost as devoted to the union movement as were their husbands. But today's younger Jewish girls show as little interest in union affairs as their Gentile sisters.

Italian immigrant families felt that the girl's place was in the home:

> The patriarchal mandate, to be "in the house after ten o'clock at night" is a factor to cope with when the union meeting lasts until midnight. In an agricultural community, . . . the woman earned money at sewing fine handiwork in the home under parents' watchful eyes. In America, . . . she is still in the shadow of the old world discipline and standards.[4]

But in a clerical local studied, the more Americanized Italian girls who entered into white-collar work showed little difference in activity from their Irish and Anglo-Saxon sisters.

Italian-speaking locals still exist in the needle trades. Here, too, there is a conflict between generations. Younger men of Italian extraction resent being "typed" and forced to attend meetings conducted in a language they hardly understand. They would like to break away, but the older generation fears that its political power might be dissipated were the locals assimilated.

This growing "Americanization" may have a serious effect on the social,

[4] Wolfson, *op. cit.*, p. 23.

cultural, and educational activities of such unions as the I.L.G.W.U. These unions are proud of the "way of life" they offer their members: their summer camps, their modern-dancing groups, their citizenship classes, and all the rest. For the recent immigrant of years past this type of service was of inestimable value. The union offered its members friendship and hospitality in a strange and inhospitable country. No wonder many of its members developed strong emotional, quasi-religious loyalties.

Today things are changing. In one situation studied, where the union had a widespread and apparently ably directed program of activities, attendance was very low. The top union officers and the older group showed great interest in the program but the younger members, for whom it was primarily designed, were apathetic.

This chapter has perhaps placed too much emphasis on the negative side of the picture, on the remaining evidence of sex and ethnic discrimination. In spite of this, the record of unions is outstandingly good. Of course, they cannot force people to drop their prejudices the minute they pass the plant gate or enter the union meeting. Nevertheless, it is safe to say that no other institution in American life has been so successful in getting men and women of different races, creeds, and nationality background to work together. Particularly within the officer group itself, members can learn to work together as individuals, not as representatives of special interest groups. And this picture of relative harmony within the local becomes even more striking when compared to the hostility and discord which exist in the very communities from which the leaders arise.

The Rank and File View
Their Union

The individuals who have held the center of attention—the officers, the stewards, and the active members who attend meetings, file and process grievances, and take part in union affairs—comprise but a small proportion of the union membership.

This chapter will deal with the inactive majority, the rank and file. It will serve the double purpose of describing their attitudes and of showing how these lead to low participation in local activities.[1]

Ambivalence Toward Union Membership

First, let us explore attitudes toward the union as an institution. The overwhelming majority of the members support the union's economic activities as useful and necessary. However, with the exception of the "active" minority, there is little interest in its internal political life.

Acceptance of its economic functions Almost every worker interviewed was sold on his union. He was convinced that he needed it for protection

[1] The analysis presented here, based on our field research, closely parallels that of Robert F. Hoxie in *Trade Unionism in the United States* (New York: Appleton-Century-Crofts, 1921), pp. 177–187.

against arbitrary management action and as an instrument for obtaining economic security. There was almost unanimous agreement that "Without a union we would be lost. The company could really take advantage of us."

The members' loyal support of their unions' economic activity is dramatically shown by the privations they have endured to win strikes—even though these were for the benefit of a small group or a plant hundreds of miles away. When a man "hits the bricks" for eighty to one hundred days he is subject to real pressure: his savings dwindle, his children are hungry, his wife often unsympathetic, and the community openly hostile. He may be bitter and antagonistic toward his union, but he seldom lets it down.

Even in new unions the picket line is almost sacred. Most members will refuse to cross one even when they think the strike unjustified. Perhaps the most striking demonstration of loyalty was shown by the union-shop elections under the Taft-Hartley Act where over 90 per cent of the workers voted to accept a union shop.

Regardless of what may have been said about worker apathy toward the union and suspicion of their officers, the essential fact of their fundamental allegiance should not be forgotten.

Absence of emotional involvement   A distinction can be made between "intellectual acceptance" of the union and "emotional identification" with it. Almost all workers were convinced of its value as a form of job security; only a minority showed "emotional identification" with its organizational goals. Dalton, drawing from participant experience in three factories, came to the same conclusion:

> Ninety percent or more of the production workers of the three plants were union members. They responded to strikes called by the national union. They showed considerable solidarity in holding production to agreed levels. However, there was a general lack of union consciousness among them.[2]

Of course, a substantial minority of members do feel such involvement. Mine and garment workers often have a devotion to their union which is almost religious. The common sacrifices of men who have been through a lot together builds up a feeling that the union is "we." One such worker said: "It is hard to explain why you are active. It's something in your heart and something in your brain."

At the other extreme are those who look upon unionism as a necessary evil. For instance, there were farmers, new to industrial life, who joined the union only because they perceived it as something required by the job. They reasoned that there were a lot of unpleasant things about factory life which they must accept, among these: getting to work on time, obeying the foreman,

[2] Melville Dalton, "Unofficial Union Management Relations," *American Sociological Review,* Vol. 15, No. 5 (October 1950), p. 612.

and joining the union. However, even such people felt that the union provided protection against immeasurable dangers. As one individual said:

> This is a good union to belong to because it is powerful in the industry. It's like hospitalization insurance. It is worth thirty bucks a year to me to make sure that nothing is going to happen.

It follows that for a member who takes such an attitude, active and personal experience as a union member is almost as remote as his membership in Blue Cross. To be sure, he "accepts" the union. He is willing to follow it in its proper sphere, to "render unto Cæsar the things that are Cæsar's," but no more anxious to exceed the necessary minimum of participation (dues-paying, striking) than he is to report to work earlier than is required.

Typical of this attitude was one member's question: "I pay my dues. Do I have to go to meetings too?" One leader called it "the nickel-in-the-slot attitude. You put your money in and maybe something comes out."

This apathy toward the union's organizational, or "internal," life shows up in participation statistics. Participation is relatively high in matters which concern the union's *collective-bargaining* function. However, participation in *internal* activities is much lower unless these are directly tied in to collective bargaining. As has been discussed, attendance at union meetings averages 2 to 8 per cent of the total membership, but extraordinary events, such as strike votes or contract negotiations, may bring out 40 to 80 per cent. Stewardships and memberships on minor committees—jobs requiring expenditure of effort with few rewards—are often hard to fill.

Or take the fact that when it is easy to vote (for instance, when the ballot box is placed at the plant gate), as high as 90 per cent of the members will take part in regular officer elections. On the other hand, if voting involves any real effort, the percentage of votes cast will depend, in part, on the extent to which economic issues are involved. Two hotly contested elections in one local resulted in a better than 60 per cent turnout, even though the operations of the company were scattered over a large metropolis and almost every member had to make a special trip to get to the polls. Without such issues, participation may fall to 20 per cent.

Origins of Ambivalence

Many of the reasons workers feel apathetic are subconscious or at best semi-conscious and, therefore, difficult to verbalize. For this reason, we made use of "projective tests," which enabled us to probe deeper into worker attitudes toward the union in general and the grievance procedure in particular. Union members were shown photographs of groups of workers, or of workers and management people, and then asked such questions as: "Here is a worker telling the other fellows about a grievance he has; what do you suppose they are thinking?" or "Here are some union officers talking over a grievance with management; what do you think they are saying?"

What we were seeking, of course, was a clearer picture of the doubts and conflicts besetting union members. Here are some of the things we found—anxieties which, though rarely expressed in words, showed up again and again in spite of basic loyalty to the union.

Shame in Accepting Help

Many workers fear that joining the union means accepting help in an area where they should be able to manage by themselves. The American ideal, and in particular the middle-class ideal, is one of self-sufficiency and individual initiative. But humiliating experiences have taught the workers that they are weak, that they must accept the union, that in effect they must surrender some of those middle-class aspirations. The result is likely to be a subconscious feeling that some degree of shame is attached to union membership and a subconscious hostility toward the union for getting them into such a dilemma.

A large proportion of workers showed considerable hesitation about using the grievance procedure as a means of settling their problems. Over and over they said, with considerable pride:

> No, I've never had a grievance, never expect to. I've never used the grievance procedure. Mostly that's used by troublemakers, people who can't settle their own problems.

Sensitivity to Community Antipathy

Doubts about unions were particularly strong in companies which had community reputations as "good places to work." Confusion is a natural result when the workers' friends and associates tell them that the company is good and the union bad but their own experiences have taught them otherwise.

This sensitivity to community feeling was found to be greatest in small towns. But even in big-city union centers a few members wince when Jimmy Hoffa takes a stand which is generally interpreted by the newspapers, press, and radio as antisocial.

For the same reason, every time their top officers are accepted by the general public as good citizens, the members as a whole are greatly pleased. They are gratified, for instance, to see newspaper photographs of their international president at a banquet with nationally known political or industrial leaders. (On the other hand, union members become anxious when their local officers get too "chummy" with local management. They seem less worried about the possibility of the international officers "selling out" to management.)

Reluctance to Attack the Company

The average worker may resent being dominated by his boss, but he is grateful for his job. This ambivalence crops up again and again. Even rabid union leaders sometimes made statements like the following:

> You've got to feel something for the company which gives you a chance to work—and gives pretty good pay.

Active members would often remark along these lines:

> Wages here may not always have been the highest, but still during good times and bad, I've had enough money to feed and clothe my family, keep up this house and send my kids through school.

Many workers felt that their present problems were only temporary. They would look back to some previous "golden age." This was a time before there had been a change in management personnel—usually when some conscientious, well-liked man was general manager or president. This man, they agreed, knew the workers and their problems. As one said:

> Under Mr. Y this was a fine company. It's this [financial district] gang which is changing things. In the old days, they'd treat you like a man.

Some believed that the only thing really wrong with the company was the personal selfishness of one or two people. "If only these were removed, things might be very different." Thus, the only purpose of the union, as they saw it, was to deal with these few obstinate individuals who refused to treat their employees like men.

Considerable feeling was expressed in the rank-and-file interviews that the company might act differently if there were no union or if the union were less aggressive. They "recalled" that just before the union came the company was all set to improve conditions. One loyal member remarked:

> We had softball teams. The company sponsored and paid for equipment for the bowling team. The rumor was they were even going to bring in an athletic director to really sponsor a lot of sports for the fellows. Well, there's no getting around it. The company didn't like the union and still doesn't, and they hold it against the men. As soon as the union came in, all that stuff went out.

Fear of Management Reprisal

Many members feared that the company would punish them if they became too active in the union:

> Many fellows feel guilty about speaking their minds at union meetings. They know the word usually gets back to management. Then they feel guilty whenever the superintendent walks through the plant and looks at them.

For one thing, we all know that no matter where you say something, whether it's at a union meeting, or at the union office, or in the plant, it all gets back to the company, and they hold it against you. Oh, you don't get fired or anything like that. When it comes to asking for something special, say a day off or something like that, the guy who hasn't done these things gets it while you get nothing. Never any privileges; never any breaks.

Other members revealed similar feelings by their reactions to the pictures of workers processing grievances. For example:

This fellow is feeling like a heel going before the company with a poor case. You can see how jittery he is.

That fellow is wondering what the outcome is going to be. You can see he's saying to himself, "I wonder what effect this is going to have on me if I lose." He thinks he's fighting a losing case. It looks as though they may have something on him too. The man in the middle—it's a company man—seems to be giving him the business. The company has the union on the spot.

Since they fear reprisal, the members want to avoid being identified with particular grievances. Yet the *officers, too,* often refuse to accept responsibility and insist that the members stand up and sign their own grievances. Naturally the workers are resentful, since they think of the union as something that will handle their relations with the company without getting them personally involved.

The members have mixed feelings over the degree of aggressiveness the union should show toward management. While the rank and file fear that they are being "sold out" when the officers fail to act vigorously, they are concerned that management will exact retribution if the officers try to take a strong stand. For example:

If the company thinks that the union is using grievances to bully them, then when negotiations come up, the company won't give in so easily. Now this last time, there must have been something that made the company stand up and be a little tougher. We didn't get as much as we should have otherwise.

The net effect is that although the members hope that most of the punishment will fall on the leaders, they fear that they themselves will be hurt to some extent. Consequently, they have an incentive to maximize their "distance" from the union; and, once again, they project their feelings in the form of hostility toward the officers of the union.

Attitudes Toward Officers

The hostility produced takes two major forms—suspicion of officers' motives and resentment of their "control."

Suspicion

In the situations studied, most union members perceived that the union was controlled by relatively few individuals. A typical comment was:

> You just get through throwing out one group and another group gets in, and before you know it there is a clique again. It's always the same, no matter how often you throw officers out, those that get in become a clique within a year and start running things to suit themselves.

They questioned their officers' motives in seeking office, their financial integrity, and their attentiveness to the real needs of the individual members:

> Bill's in it just for what he can get for himself. He gets that extra twenty dollars a month and a few hours lost time, and a good many of those are cooked up.
>
> Mac took it because of what they did to him last year. He figured that this is the best way to get back at the guys that took his seniority away.

On the other hand, few of the men were willing to accept union office.

> You have all those meetings to go to. You never have any time with your family. You've always got some guy around your neck who is after something he doesn't deserve.

Because union office is so undesirable, the average member seems to feel that no one would take it unless he could "get something out of it for himself," either in terms of a better job, improved seniority, nepotistic influence, or personal power.

Particularly in a larger plant, malicious rumors circulate from department to department. They seem to have little relation to reality—yet all are warped to show that the union has "sold out" or that the officers are incompetent or greedy.

Yet, our experience indicates that these suspicions were hardly ever justified. In one plant, for instance, nearly every officer was accused by one group or another of having used his position to obtain favored seniority status. In fact, however, over half the active leadership worked on the most undesirable shift. Rank-and-file members constantly said that their officers were "getting too much," when in fact their modest remuneration hardly covered out-of-pocket losses incurred in functioning as a union officer.

Geoffrey Gorer offers an insight which may help explain these suspicions. He suggests that Americans have a common tendency to discredit those who hold political office:

> A person who goes into a political career for reasons other than direct personal advantage is deeply suspect; he is perhaps secretly lusting after authority—and the greatest vigilance must be exercised to see that he does not gratify this sinful craving.
>
> The government is apart from the people; its interests are different from

the interests of the community; the main aim of the government is to increase its authority, and the main aim of the public is to resist it.[3]

Americans are used to thinking in terms of political bosses. The union member does not find it difficult to transfer his caricature of the ward leader from the community into the plant. In the union, active participants are sometimes looked upon with suspicion.

This suspicion is accentuated by the fact that the ideology of a union is equalitarian. In most local meetings, it is customary to refer to other members as "brother;" officers regularly use the term in everyday conversation. Nevertheless, the union needs to create a hierarchy of officers, a system of inequality. In a way, the officers are forced to violate their own moral code—and the rank and file are quick to seize on this as an opportunity to vent their aggressions:

> Every time you elect someone, he stops being one of you and starts throwing his weight around. That's the way people are—but I wouldn't take a union job.

Such deep-felt attitudes cannot be hidden from the officer group. They respond with feelings of martyrdom and self-importance. Their complaints often run in these terms:

> Look what I've done for the boys, all the help I've given them. I never get a cent of pay—I never get a word of thanks. After all I've done, I don't understand how they can say things like that.

Executive board meetings sometimes broke down into general "crying sessions" during which the leaders exchanged stories about the rank-and-file abuse they had taken. There was much talk of "protecting" officers from "this type of abuse," although little was ever done.

In turn, the rank and file were quick to note in the behavior of their officers this self-righteous attitude toward the membership. In a way, this process was circular. The antagonism of each group increased that of the other.

These feelings could be directed against the union but, since most members are clearly convinced of the union's value, it is psychologically safer to express them against the officers, particularly if, as Gorer suggests, the officers are culturally approved scapegoats. For many members, this ambivalence of attitude is resolved by saying: "The union is good—it's the officers who are spoiling it."

Resentment of officer's "control"   Chapter 2 has illustrated how the union's relationship with management is a dynamic one, developing in many cases from the hostile to the harmonious. As it changes, the relationship between

[3] Geoffrey Gorer, *The American Character* (London: The Crescent Press, 1948), pp. 22–23.

the union and the rank and file must change too. This factor is often forgotten.

We have seen how, in the organizing period, the protest elements of the union are emphasized; its function is to protect the workers against the arbitrary whims of management. So, at first, the average worker expects the union to be "for" him and the company to be "against" him. He looks upon the union as his lawyer—as an organization which will fight for his interests, right or wrong.

Frequently he is disappointed in his expectations. In eliminating arbitrary decision-making, the union agrees to rules. From that time on, grievances must be framed in terms of these rules. The union can no longer be "agin" everything.

Unions, in their attempt to restrict the exercise of management prerogatives, have taken upon themselves the responsibility of making day-to-day decisions that involve choices between groups within the rank and file. Here it is totally impossible for the officers to satisfy everyone.

In five of the locals studied, the unions accepted partial responsibility for a job evaluation program. In each, the workers were skeptical of its scientific nature. They were sure that the jobs could easily be made to "go up" or "go down" whenever the union or company officials desired.

In most of the situations studied, the union took major responsibility for the administering of seniority. In effect, management seemed to say: "This is your baby and it's up to you to make it work." Naturally, seniority disputes gave rise to charges of discrimination. It was said that the officers made their decisions on the basis of favoritism. Often it was rumored that officers accepted union office only to change seniority in their own favor.

Many considerations inhibit the officers from pushing even purely anti-company grievances to the hilt. They realize that the union's bargaining position is limited—if they win one grievance they lessen their chances of winning another. Few grievances can be considered purely on their own merits. For these reasons the officers must somehow devise techniques by which they can screen out grievances they feel should not be pushed: they formalize the grievance procedure and require each case to run an obstacle course before it gets to management.

Few members are aware of the officers' problems. When their grievances are sidetracked or turned down, they are inclined to attribute this to favoritism, cowardice, and incompetence. The formality of the grievance procedure is viewed with particular suspicion. The members cannot understand how their simple complaints can become so enmeshed in a mass of red tape. Often members describe their hearings before the executive board in terms such as these:

> You can be damn sure the cards are stacked against you every time you go before them. All they want to do is wriggle out of the contract. Sweezy

[the local president] treats you colder than McGuire [the personnel manager].

Now when Ames was president, it was like going to the Supreme Court. He thought he was a judge. I took a case to him and he told me what the hell to expect; the company had been too good to me as it was.

They're always trying to find precedents. No matter what it is, it's been decided before—against you.

Naturally such quotes came from the more verbal complainers. Others felt: "What's the use? A grievance causes a lot of trouble, and it doesn't get you anywhere." Or as a worker responded to a projective photograph:

The fellow [in the picture] is saying to himself: "I'm all by myself. If I make a mistake, I'm out altogether." You've got to choose your words carefully at those meetings. They're just waiting for you to make a stumble and then they've got you.

In some situations, where the union was particularly strong, the workers perceived it as great a barrier to winning a grievance as management. Workers in these situations would say:

The company likes it better now. The union handles the men.
Once the union *agrees* to fight for you, it usually wins.
Our steward tried to keep peace. He is just sort of in the middle between the worker and the company. He looks at both sides.

Previous chapters have discussed how participation in union activities was correlated with economic success within the union. Members of low-participation groups commented:

It doesn't pay to fight. The union is against you from the start.
They [the officers] think you are making too much anyway and they aren't interested in helping you.
The union is really for the production workers. We just pay our dues.

In summary then, "working harmony" or "industrial peace" means that the union official accepts increasing responsibility in areas at one time under the sole control of management. In turn, the official becomes charged by the members with additional responsibility for working conditions. Increasingly, members tend to vent upon the union some of the feelings which would otherwise be directed against management. Thus, wherever the union is strongly organized the worker perceives his working conditions as to some extent being determined by *both* the union and the company.

Conclusion

Under normal circumstances, rank-and-file members are willing to devote little time to the union's internal political activities. This, is in sharp contrast to the active members' participation. For the inactive members, the union is a formal institution; for the active ones it is an informal social group as well.

For a small group the union is a way of life. For the majority it is but a method of representation—although an important one. The leaders are so wrapped up in their union that it has almost become an end in itself. This is not true for the rank and file. For them it is but a means to an end, a way of gaining greater security on the job, not a great social movement.

The vast majority of the members readily accept the union's economic functions but deny its social purpose. They do not become involved in the inner life of the local and so fail to gain the social satisfactions of membership. Thus, this is really a circular process.

There is hostility toward the union for the aspects of "control" it assumes—and suspicion of the power given to the leader. Added to this are the guilt and fear surrounding any attack on management, and shame in not being able to stand up for ones self to fulfill the American ideal. As a result, many members look upon unions as a *necessary evil*—with all the ambivalence that such a phrase connotes.

Nevertheless, the average member does recognize participation in union activities as a considerable social obligation. Knowing he ought to attend meetings more often, he feels something of the guilt of a man in a small town who refuses to join the volunteer fire department. He is forced therefore to rationalize an excuse, which may be tied in with what Herberg calls a "psychic cleavage" between two concepts of the union's basic function:

> A modern labor union is, at one and the same time, (1) a business-like service organization, operating a variety of agencies under a complicated system of industrial relations; and (2) an expression and vehicle of the historical movement of the submerged laboring masses for social recognition and democratic self-determination.[4]

This "psychic cleavage" is seized upon by the members as their "out." If the union were really a social movement, then they would have to participate. But of course it isn't, they reason; it is only a business organization, and so there is no need to attend meetings or engage in other internal activities. Consequently, the average members tend to look upon the union as "they," as a highly important form of insurance, as an agency which, with all its limitations, will provide certain types of protection—for a fee.

Looking at his union in this way, the rank-and-file member is not being disloyal. In fact, his feelings toward his union parallel those of Mr. Average U.S. Citizen toward his government. He grudgingly pays his taxes and has little interest in working politics, unless there is a particularly colorful scandal. He rarely attends town meetings and is unconcerned with the "nasty"

[4] Will Herberg, "Bureaucracy and Democracy in Labor Unions," *The Antioch Review*, Vol. 3, No. 3 (Autumn 1943), p. 406.

fighting which characterizes much of political activity. On election day he votes only if the issues are dramatized enough and if it isn't too much trouble. In short, he normally acts only when his particular interests are being neglected. (But when war comes, he shows real patriotism and a sense of unity with fellow citizens.)

Most of the time both union and government are considered necessary evils. Like the policeman, the business agent should come in a hurry when called and the rest of the time "keep the hell away." The rank-and-file member is a patriotic citizen but leaves routine work to others—"they are paid for it, aren't they?"

14

Are Unions Democratic?

Definitions are always a problem, particularly where the term is invested with as much emotion as is the word "democracy." A common approach to this subject stresses the union's constitutional structure. According to this view, every union is democratic if its constitution provides machinery whereby the members can change their officers and determine basic union policy. By this criterion, few unions are undemocratic!

Another approach is to look at union democracy from the point of view of participation in union politics. This approach considers questions such as: How many candidates are there in elections? How often is there a turnover in officers? Are there organized political parties? How much disagreement is there at meetings, and what is the average attendance at them? Were locals required to meet all these criteria, we would find few democratic.

Both approaches are somewhat limited. Both are concerned only with the superficial, or most easily measurable, indicators of democracy. Many people evaluate unions unconsciously in terms of the town meeting. They feel that unless everyone participates actively there is no democracy. Yet, as we have seen, in most locals the important decisions are made behind the scenes, in meetings of the executive and grievance committees, at informal discussions among the officers, and during casual contacts between the officers and rank and file in the plant. The local meeting is primarily a ceremony to ratify decisions made elsewhere.

From the point of view of our study, union democracy can best be measured in terms of the responsiveness of the officers to the demands of the members. A good way to evaluate this form of democracy is through the attitudes of the membership. How free do the workers feel to express their grievances or complaints? What is the average member's estimate of his chances of being heard by the officers and of having something done about his particular problem? How well do union policies reflect the views of the rank and file?

If we apply such a definition of democracy, we may utilize such criteria as these: the ability of member-interest groups to use internal union pressures (rather than self-help techniques) to obtain favorable consideration of their grievances; the extent to which important questions of policy enter into union elections; the degree to which officers can combine the roles of administrator with those of the social leader; the vigor of the stewards; and the effectiveness of the grievance procedure as a line of communication.

Of course, informal channels of communication can be easily blocked unless there is an ever present possibility that "poor service" will result in grievances being aired in a membership meeting or at the ballot box. In general, democracy of the sort we are speaking of functions effectively only as a corollary of lively meetings and contested elections.

Why Union Democracy is Important

If democracy flourishes on the face-to-face level, the chances are greater that it will flourish in the nation as a whole. Roughly 25 per cent of the labor force in the United States consists of union members. For the most part, they do not have the opportunity to participate in the traditionally middle-class service organizations which bulk so important in training community leaders. Democratic unions encourage individual expression and self-development and thus train democratic citizens.

Union democracy is equally important from the standpoint of enlightened management. One reason workers join unions is to express their grievances. They want to speak with a voice which management will hear. The union is their channel of communication with management. When grievances are hidden, discontent festers and saps the morale of the workers and the strength of the productive enterprise.

Democracy is also preferable from the point of view of the union organizer who is interested solely in maximizing the effectiveness of his union. Without democracy, particpation falls off. Even if the dues stream continues, identification with the organization is impaired. This may well affect worker solidarity when there is no strike.

Without democracy, there is no way of discovering good leaders within the rank and file who will donate their services and gain the confidence of their fellows. Without such leaders, the organization is crippled, for the paid officers cannot do all the work.

The Local is More Democratic than the International

Many authors have been discouraged about the future of union democracy. They deplore the concentration of power in the hands of a few leaders who are never defeated in elections, and they deplore the paucity of discussion on basic union policy. In most cases, their conclusions are based on studies of the Internationals. Our own research has been on the local level, and here we find that conditions are better for both participation and communication.

The vitality of the local lies in its relatively simple organization; its work can be done by men off duty or on lost time. Because of the officers' daily contact with the rank and file, their effectiveness and responsiveness can be directly evaluated. This is particularly true in grievance-handling. Of course, a few industrial locals have paid business agents, but even these can be easily supervised by unpaid executive committees composed of men working in the shop.

In local elections, the informal nominating procedure and the ease of voting contribute to relatively high participation and a large number of candidates. The ever present possibility of being defeated spurs the officers to alertness.

The International bureaucracy contrasts sharply with the responsiveness of the local officers. The International requires, and can afford, a team of paid professional experts: organizers, field representatives, education directors, research economists, statisticians, and actuaries. These "porkchoppers" do not have regular contact with the rank and file and once in office are extremely hard to oust. Most utilize highly specialized skills that the rank and file can neither understand nor directly oversee.

To the unpaid union leader, his office is just another form of leisure-time activity; to the porkchopper it is a livelihood. Of course, if defeated, most porkchoppers can go back to the shops, but as A. J. Muste asks:

> How many people will one encounter in a year's travel who can bring themselves to exchange a white-collar official position for a dirty, monotonous, hot, exacting obscure wage-slave's job in a mine or mill?[1]

Not only will he fight harder to keep his office, but his means of doing so will be more effective. The local president who must manage his campaign in his spare time has little advantage over his opponent. But this advantage

[1] A. J. Muste, "Factional Fights in Trade Unions," *American Labor Dynamics,* J. B. S. Hardman, Ed. (New York: Harcourt, Brace & World, 1928), p. 341.

increases enormously once he goes on the full-time payroll as an International officer. The mere fact that he occupies a focal point of communications gives him a commanding lead over those who would clip his wings. Added to this are other sources of strength, as Reynolds enumerates:

> The methods used are those of machine politics anywhere. The union leader makes friends with as many members of the organization as he can, performs various services for them, distributes salaried positions in the right quarters, uses the union newspaper to present himself in a favorable light, stage-manages the union conventions, and makes full use of oratory and the other political arts. All this he does in perfectly good faith. He becomes convinced after a few years that he can run the union better than anyone else, and in many cases, he is right.[2]

To a much greater extent than is possible in governmental politics, the International administration personifies the union. It can "educate" the rank and file to think of the administration and the union as somehow identical. It can make them think that a vote against the administration is also a vote against the union and everything it stands for. It can extol its own activities in "building" the union and protecting the organization from its enemies and it can castigate the "destructive" activities of the opposition.

Furthermore, the average member has no standard by which to judge whether the International president does a good job in his nation-wide activities, but he has well-informed opinions about how his grievanceman handles problems in the plant.

An informed public opinion can be better developed on the local level than on the International. Except in locals of 10,000 or more members or in polyglot locals consisting of many small shops, the interested members (and more particularly the active leaders) can rely on face-to-face contacts to maintain communications. The work of the local gets a thorough going over whether the men meet at the workplace, at the plant gate, in the plant cafeteria, or at the neighborhood bar.

With all its shortcomings, the local membership meeting is still an effective forum for group discussion. In spite of much confusion, it affords ample opportunity for the members to criticize their officers. And in times of crisis, when alternatives are clearly defined, it does make decisions.

On the International level, the ability of members to exchange opinions and place pressure on the leadership is limited:

> As in modern corporations and the government bureau, the relations between the leaders of the national union and the individual workers in the shop may become tenuous sometimes to the point of extinction.

[2] Lloyd Reynolds, *Labor Economics and Labor Relations* (Englewood Cliffs, New Jersey: Prentice-Hall, Inc., 1949), p. 147.

. . . There are a variety of levels of organizational authority in the typical union, and whatever influence the individual worker can exert must frequently be filtered through the complicated delegation-of-power system. . . . The worker must rely on the intelligence and honesty of persons delegated to represent him, and these delegates in turn must authorize a still smaller group (usually the national officers) to act for the union.[3]

Certainly the existence of a large number of "layers" between the rank and file and the International officers makes it more difficult for the officers to know what the rank-and-file members want and for the rank-and-file members to control the officers.

The administration of the International can mend its fences and consolidate support fifty-two weeks a year, but the opposition must wait for the few caucuses in the early days of the International convention before making its plans. Prior to that, contact must often be made by letter or mimeographed "opposition bulletin." While the administration is always able to use official publicity for its purposes, many unions prohibit the publication of opposition newspapers or the formation of opposition factions.

Consequently, even if the opposition is not driven underground, it is forced to become conspiratorial. The semihysterical attacks to which it must resort in order to gain attention are no match for the friendly handshake of the International representative or the slick-paper journal written by the professional publicity man.

In general, then, locals are more democratic than their parent Internationals. In fact, a majority of those we examined maintained an energetic political life, with lively (although often poorly directed) debate in their meetings and a substantial turnover of officers. Although only a small proportion of the members were active in union affairs, there was nothing to prevent others becoming more active if they wished. There were many opportunities for dissatisfied members to protest decisions—even more than those specified in the contract grievance procedure. A determined member could take his case to many different levels of the local hierarchy.

Loss of Initial Democratic Enthusiasm

Most new locals start life being democratic and then go through a period of decline in which they lose some of their youthful vigor. However, this decline goes further in some locals than in others. Looking back at previous chapters, we can outline the reasons for both this initial decline in democracy and for the eventual development of some sort of equilibrium, where forces

[3] Frank C. Pierson, "The Government of Trade Unions," *Industrial and Labor Relations Review,* Vol. 1, No. 4 (July 1948), p. 595.

toward and away from democracy are balanced. Finally, we will try to suggest reasons why some locals are more democratic than others.

Decline in Participation

Immediately after a new union is organized, interest is high, and this is reflected in meeting attendance, as it is in other union activities. But once the original excitement has passed and the first contract is signed, meetings become increasingly dull. Attendance picks up when the contract is being negotiated or a strike is imminent, but there is a tendency for negotiations to become less dramatic. As relations with management become more "mature," there is less to fight about.

The leaders learn that their task will be easier and they will be subject to fewer pressures if they keep reasonably quiet about what happens at the bargaining table. Since they no longer rush to the membership to report and ask instructions, the rank and file loses its sense of vicarious participation in contract and grievance bargaining. Thus, meeting attendance tends to decline until it reaches a stable median (from 2 to 8 per cent in the locals we studied). Aside from a few lonely isolates and departmental representatives, the "hard core" becomes increasingly narrowed down to leaders and their followers.

Provided it does not take too much time, a large portion of the members still go through the motions of voting in officer elections. However, as the union loses its novelty, their interest and excitement decline. Increasingly, the members say, "The man who is now in is doing a good job, so why kick him out?" or "The new man will be just as bad." Although election upsets may take place, there is an observable trend toward concentration of leadership among the top-status groups.

The Leaders and the Rank and File Become Two Groups

When the union is new, its leaders are anxious to recruit people to help them. Anyone with sufficient time and energy can participate, not only in the ratification of decisions already made but in the decision-making process itself. But as it grows older a twofold change takes place. The leaders tend to restrict the number with whom they consult before making a decision; the rank and file increasingly look upon the officers as "they" rather than "we"— a group separate and distinct from themselves.

Previous chapters have explained rank-and-file suspicion of their officers. It is natural that the officers should be aware of this feeling. In turn, they resent the passivity of the membership, their willingness to sit back and criticize while the officers do all the work.

They begin to doubt the sincerity of members who are "too greedy." They say:

> Sometimes I wonder whether this democracy is really worth the cost. They [the members] don't want leaders, they want messenger boys. No wonder some of those guys [leaders of undemocratic unions] get hard [unresponsive].

In spite of sharp differences among themselves, the leaders enter into a tacit agreement to protect each other in public. They accentuate their isolation further in order to protect themselves from "pressures" brought to bear on grievance cases.

Decline in Communication

In most instances, the new union is organized by a coalition of "natural leaders." But once in power, these natural leaders have a tendency to freeze out any young upstart who challenges them. As this clique excludes a larger and larger proportion of these leaders, it begins to lose contact with the rank and file. In theory, the shop steward should be the intermediary between the officers and the rank and file. In practice, as we have seen, his decline in prestige and authority also reduces his value as a communications link.

In this way, the communications channels within the union tend to dry up. The rank and file feel less free to bring their problems to the officers; the officers are less interested in hearing them. Members take the increasingly fatalistic attitude that voting and attending meetings are useless. Few are willing to run for office. There is little interest in other forms of union activity.

Of course, such developments are uneven. Some groups still find that participation "pays off," while others feel that they are the forgotten minority. And of those who feel left out, some resort to self-help measures, and others become apathetic.

Such, then, is the discouraging story of the way many locals lose part of their democracy. Some locals might carry this process further, say to the point where officers completely abolish elections and meetings without the rank and file objecting. But none of the locals studied went this far. In every case, there were checks which seemed to prevent any further decline of democracy—even if the officers had so desired.

Checks on Declines in Democracy

Without question, the tradition of the union movement itself is a strong force favoring democracy. The vast majority of leaders became interested in unionism precisely because of their dedication to democratic principles. In most instances, they would rather be defeated in a fair election than win an unfair one. They are proud of their union's democracy; many officers take a wry pride in the amount of opposition they receive.

But even if the officers were not committed to the democratic ethic, rank-and-file attitudes would help to keep them in line. Although the general attitude of the rank-and-file worker is "Let George do it," there is a hidden string. What he really means is "Let George do it as long as George delivers the goods." Since economic conditions are variable, George cannot deliver indefinitely. When the union faces reverses, George will have unpleasant news—for instance, that the men will have to go out on strike or that they will have to accept a pay cut.

At this point the relationship between the leaders and the membership becomes important. If the leadership has maintained its lines of communication, its explanations will be accepted and the rank and file will stand by loyally. But if the lines of communication have become clogged, then these members will be suspicious, restless, and resentful—they will lose confidence in their leaders.

What does the rank and file do when it loses confidence in its leaders? It has a number of alternatives, the most obvious being to vote for a new slate of officers at the next elections. Of course, as described in a previous chapter, economic factors rarely enter into such elections, but when they do, the toll among incumbents is great.

This assumes that the local maintains the formal trimmings of procedural democracy. It assumes, for instance, that if a member attacks the officers in a meeting he will not be subject to retaliation, that regular elections are held, that nominations are free, that all are given a chance to vote, and that the ballots are counted fairly. Even in the small minority of locals in which the leadership met no apparent opposition, these minimal protections were provided.

Suppose, however, that the dissatisfied members are unsuccessful at the polls or that the leadership is somehow able to restrict the exercise of procedural rights. What prevents these locals from going all the way to one-man rule?

Even in dictatorial unions workers have grievances. If the officers do not react to the normal "internal" pressures previously discussed, the workers still have a final recourse: following their "informal" leaders, they can resort to wildcat strikes, work restriction, and other forms of self-help. What better way for the members to express their frustration than to go on a spontaneous strike? But this is highly dangerous for the union administration, for if the *official* leaders cannot call off the strike, management will deal with the leaders who can.

Even if resentment against the union leadership leads to neither an election battle nor self-help activities, it may result in apathy. And too great apathy is dangerous both to the union and to its leaders. A union's strength depends upon the loyalty of its rank and file and the number and ability of its active participants. Without an active group of unpaid leaders the union may fall apart—the paid full-time officials just can't do all the work. Apathy loses strikes. And when there is no union shop, it results in loss of members and the disintegration of locals. Even with a union shop an apathetic local is easy prey for any competing International with a penchant for raiding.

All these possibilities scare the average leader. Of course, he is already strongly committed to democracy as a system of values, but he learns along the way that it also builds a stronger union. Looked at from another point of view, unions with sound human-relations structures will be able to solve tougher problems than those where human relations are weak.

Situational Determinants of Democracy

As we have pointed out, some locals are more democratic than others. All unions are buffeted by the forces discussed above—yet why does their dynamic balancing sometimes result in an active, highly participating local and other times in one whose members are completely apathetic? In order to seek a further answer to this question, we will list *some* of the situational factors that influence the union's internal life. Of course, in any given instance, some of these may be exceedingly important and others of negligible significance.

Locus of Control

To the extent that the "locus of control" over collective bargaining is concentrated in the International, rank-and-file opportunity to participate is reduced. Most unions which sign multiplant agreements provide for membership votes before demands are submitted or the contract ratified, but at best this type of participation is not satisfactory. It makes a tremendous amount of difference if one of the members of the negotiating committee is a man from your shop from whom you can get the "straight dope" as to what is happening—who will even give you an eyewitness account of how the superintendent lost his temper and how the International representative made the company president eat dirt.

To the workers in one automobile plant studied, the 1950 wage agreement came as a complete surprise. A few knew that negotiations were in process, but their chief source of information was the daily paper. Consequently, there was almost no feeling of involvement in the negotiations.

In another plant, the local did its own negotiating. In this plant, the situation was entirely different. In large departments, every worker had a good picture of what happened within a few hours after each negotiation session broke up. Consequently, the officers were continually able to sound out their constituents as to the relative importance of different demands—and to prepare them for necessary concessions.

But it must be emphasized once again that contract negotiations are only part of the picture. Even where contracts are negotiated on a country-wide basis, the rank and file may exercise considerable influence over the processing of grievances.

Negotiations on the local level are not an automatic guarantee of rank-and-file participation. In locals in service and craft industries which must bargain with many small firms, most of the negotiations are conducted by the business agents without extensive membership participation. Since the firms are highly competitive, the business agent must spend most of his time preventing "chiseling" on the standard rate for the job. Therefore, he has little opportunity to handle other types of grievances—and rank-and-file opportunities to communicate are circumscribed.

History and Organization of the Union

The formal structure of the International and the unwritten traditions which lie behind this have a definite effect upon the local, for the law and its interpretations are intricately entwined.

Although Hoxie's division of unions into functional types is far less relevant now than it was in the 1920's,[4] echoes of the past constantly reverberate in the union's present. Since all unions are basically mutual self-help associations, they all have some tradition of democracy. But the tradition is far stronger in formerly "uplift" unions like the I.L.G.W.U. than in "business" unions like the Carpenters. To be sure, apathy at the rank-and-file level is characteristic of many locals in clothing unions, but the clothing union officers observed consistently reaffirmed their belief in democracy, in striking contrast to business agents of many "business unions." In the same way, the U.A.W.'s sad experience with Homer Martin (its first president and would-be dictator) did much to cement its democratic tradition.

Even the new local inherits a wealth of tradition from the International. The auto locals we studied were located far from Detroit, yet the democracy they showed probably reflected conditions there. In one newly formed local of another C.I.O. International, the members were told again and again by the International president and the International representative, "in the C.I.O. we don't do things that way."[5]

[4] Robert F. Hoxie, *Trade Unionism in the United States* (New York: Appleton-Century-Crofts, 1921), pp. 44–52. Hoxie describes four "functional" types: business unions, uplift unions, revolutionary unions, predatory unions.

[5] Among the suggestions which met this treatment were: (1) that seniority demands be decided by mail referendum, (2) that shop stewards dispose of grievances by themselves, or submit them to the third stage without executive board approval, (3) that shop stewards as a body be given certain legislative powers.

Unions which have been organized "from the top down" by the International may show less political activity than those built "bottom up" from self-organized locals.

The role of historical accident should not be forgotten. In one situation we studied, the NLRB split the workers into two separate units: clerical and production. The stock record clerks were placed in the clerical unit, although they might easily have been placed in the production unit. Since this group was made up of the most active and able leaders in the company, it easily established control over the clerical local. As a consequence, its political life was far less turbulent than that of its sister local. Perhaps, had the NLRB ruled otherwise, the production local would have been the inactive one.

Structure

It has already been suggested that participation declines proportionally as the size of the local increases. Any factor which increases the size of the local will make participation that much more difficult.

The size of the local is often determined by the size of the plant unit. Some International constitutions require that locals be large enough to support a business agent. Even in areas with large concentrations of members, this requirement can make the local large enough to be unwieldy. Where members are spread over a broad geographical area, it makes attendance by more than a small proportion unlikely, if not impossible.

Certainly this was the case in a Teamsters local whose jurisdiction extended from central Pennsylvania to the southern tip of New Jersey. Compare the effect on democracy of this structure with that of the International Typographers' Union, where every workplace is organized into a chapel.

Local 688, a giant Teamsters local comprising 10,000 members in the St. Louis area, has taken drastic action to cut down the effect of size. Instead of one large meeting for the entire local, at which attendance doubtless would be small, meetings are held on a "shop" or industry basis, and local-wide policy is formulated by the executive committee and a shop stewards' council.

Much of the union politicking revolves around officers' elections. The more frequent the election the greater the interest. Other things being equal, one would expect locals whose officers serve short terms to be more democratic than those with long terms.

Geography

The Western Federation of Miners and the I.W.W. were in the best rip-roaring western tradition. Small-town craft locals are very different animals from their big-city brothers. As one International representative explained:

> It's been my experience that you get more interest in small town locals than in the big city. In a big city, you have all the troubles of travel to the meeting hall, and no matter what we can offer them, they get better entertainment at the shows.

Autocratic union leaders can exist in some industries without rank-and-file support if they have the aid of the local government. In some craft unions particularly, there is evidence pointing to a close tie-in between "dictatorial" union leaders and corrupt city bosses.

Character of Work Groups

Chapter 13 discussed how status, cohesiveness, and homogeneity of work groups affected relative participation of departments. It might be expected that these same factors would affect the over-all level of participation within local unions.

Following this reasoning, we can list some of the factors which we would expect to be favorable to democracy: whether the members work close together in one location instead of being spread out over a large area where they cannot communicate with one another; whether all have a similar ethnic background; whether they earn roughly the same pay; whether they are relatively highly skilled; and whether they comprise a stable work force. Each of these factors contributes to higher participation in the union and, other things being equal, to greater democracy.

One additional factor should be mentioned: certain industries seem to attract workers who have had more experience with democratic procedure than others. Members of white-collar locals often have considerable education. Education gives a man confidence to express himself; it makes him less frightened of the complex and frequently technical matters which daily confront the union. Lipset cites the high educational level of the Typographers as contributing to their democratic traditions and two-party system.[6]

A local of engineers we studied provided another example of this. Discussing a draft of their constitution, the members made continual references such as: "In organizations to which I belong . . ." or "In my experience . . ."

In contrast to this, pandemonium reigned in early meetings of a newly organized production local because few members knew even the rudiments of parliamentary procedures. Later, when they had learned it, they played with it like a toy, tying themselves up in endless procedural knots.

---

[6] Seymour Lipset, Martin Trow, and James Coleman, *Union Democracy* (New York: Doubleday & Co., Anchor Books, 1962).

The Collective-Bargaining Relationship

The collective-bargaining relationship has its effects upon the internal life and democracy of the union, an effect which may be as important as any of those so far discussed. Much of the continuing research interest in collective bargaining has been concentrated on factors contributing to industrial peace as opposed to industrial conflict. While generally considered to be a desirable social goal, we can now ask what is the impact of such industrial peace on union democracy? Does one strengthen the other, or are they mutually exclusive alternatives between which society must choose?

As we have noted, Muste suggests that the union has two conflicting functions, that of an army and that of a town meeting, and one tends to interfere with the other. It would follow that, when the union is at war, political democracy should be curtailed, for criticism of the war itself, of the objectives for which it is fought, and even of the leaders and their tactics, becomes high treason.

Although victory requires unity, and perhaps even the suppression of too-violent disagreement, can we say that the reverse is true? Does democracy flourish best under peace and security? Clyde Summers would seem to think so:

> As long as a union operates under a constant fear and anticipation of having to battle the employer for economic gains, it is bound to look upon any activity within the union which creates dissension or division, not merely as an exercise of democratic rights, but as a threat to its safety. The Typographical Union has been able to develop and maintain a two-party system with conventions, nominations, platforms, and free campaigning on the issues and the candidates. It may be more than coincidence that this union was fully accepted by the employer and did not have to strike to obtain its objectives for 25 years.[7]

But much of the evidence seems to point in the opposite direction. Some of the most enthusiastically democratic unions are those which until recently have been fighting for their lives. In many instances, good relations with management have been associated with a decline in democracy.

As long as such an "armed truce" relationship continues, in which the parties believe their major objectives are in conflict,[8] the union must be kept in fighting trim. If it wishes to retain the support of the rank and file during strikes, it must respond quickly to their needs. It must develop a strong body of noncommissioned officers in the stewards. Member grievances will be

---

[7] "Disciplinary Powers of Unions," *Industrial and Labor Relations Review,* Vol. 3, No. 4 (July 1950), p. 491. Lipset, Trow, and Coleman, *op. cit.,* seem to agree.

[8] Frederick H. Harbison and John R. Coleman, *Goals and Strategy in Collective Bargaining* (New York: Harper & Row, 1951), p. 20.

pushed with extra vigor, first, because the union cannot afford to antagonize members and second, because each grievance is a weapon in the battle.

Apathetic locals cannot win long strikes, suffer from declining membership, and are fair game for rival unions. Other things being equal, we might then expect undemocratic locals to be those which are relatively sheltered from the threats of long strikes, declining membership, and competing unions. If this is true, the possibility of extensive strikes, the open shop, and the presence of rival unions are all favorable to union democracy.

On the other hand, the greatest concentration of undemocratic unions exists where they are strong enough to "stabilize" the industry. Most of these industries are highly competitive, and the employer unit is relatively small. Some of these unions enjoy unparalleled security; yet, as Lens points out:

> In craft unions with a closed shop contract, he [the member] is dependent to a large extent on the business agent for his jobs and for the choice of jobs. To oppose official policy, particularly in the face of overwhelming odds, is definitely to jeopardize his livelihood and possibly force himself out of the union entirely.[9]

The most dangerous situations of all occur in the small minority of cases in which basic disagreement is impossible because the union and the employer have apparently reached collusive agreement. Under these circumstances, there is little need for rank-and-file support; the stimulus of external danger is at a minimum.

"Working harmony" is another form of industrial peace. In contrast to the situations where the union is stronger than the employer, parties of roughly equal strength develop a "mature" relationship in which:

> Employer and union leaders look upon collective bargaining more as a means of working together than as a competitive struggle for power. In such cases, the union-management relationship provided machinery not merely for compromising conflicting interests, but also for advancing the common or joint interests of the parties involved.[10]

Some of the problems created for the union by this new maturity have been discussed in previous chapters. When the union places a positive value on maintaining good relations with management, the officers must take responsibility for such unpleasant tasks as preserving rank-and-file discipline (through preventing wildcat strikes and other self-help techniques), screening grievances, resolving intergroup disputes (particularly in areas like seniority and job evaluation). Under some circumstances this may lead to a decline in communication and, as a consequence, the separation of the membership into two distinct groups: officers and rank and file. The long-run

[9] Sidney Lens, *Left, Right and Center* (Hinsdale, Ill.: Henry Regnery Co., 1949), p. 106.
[10] Harbison and Coleman, *op. cit.,* p. 53.

consequences of this may well be a general reduction in the members' interest and participation in the union.

Conclusion

In spite of apathy (on the part of the rank and file) and concentration of power (in the hands of the officers), the vast majority of the locals studied were essentially democratic. They are a wholesome influence upon our society. The opportunity they give to their members to express themselves is an important contribution to the American way of life.

What of tomorrow? Will a more general acceptance of working harmony result in general membership apathy? Will the union become just another bureaucratic organization?

We are guardedly optimistic. Working harmony provides its own incentives for greater membership activity. The expansion of the grievance procedure and the growing influence of the union in plant affairs mean that the net effect of the local upon the lives of its members is increasing. The members have a larger stake in keeping tabs on their officers and more to lose by being inactive. Thus, along with increased dependence upon the officers, the rank and file may well develop greater interest in controlling them.

We may, then, conclude that the possibilities for democracy are less a function of the degree of industrial peace than they are of the number of problems which the rank and file can help to solve. If democratic unionism is to survive, it must constantly meet new challenges. Thus, although the development of harmonious labor-management relationships creates new problems for the union leadership, it also provides an opportunity for broadening the range of decisions in which the worker can participate, and thus it expands the concept of industrial democracy itself.

Epilogue

Changes Since 1951

By 1951 the typical union was already ten to fifteen years old, having been founded in the late 1930's or early 40's. Having weathered the stresses which accompanied their original organization and having gone through the bitter period of the post-World War II strikes, they had now obtained a fair degree of security and seemed to be entering a period of "working harmony."

The nation was near full employment in 1951 (due in part to the Korean War); television was spreading and McCarthyism was just beginning—two developments which apparently were to effect unions greatly.

What changes have occurred since 1951?[1]

Loss of Urgency

To some extent the labor movement is no longer a *movement,* it seems to have lost its forward direction. Labor's very success, some have argued, has tended to make unions less necessary: increased wages have given workers middle-class standards, while better human relations have eliminated

[1] This section is adopted from George Strauss, "The Changing Power Balance in the Plant," *Industrial Relations,* Vol. 1, No. 3 (May, 1962), pp. 65–96.

much of the tyranny on the job. Consequently, traditional union objectives have become outmoded.

This point of view may be easily exaggerated. Yet it is undoubtedly true that many union leaders have lost their sense of missionary zeal; like most individual Americans, unions today show little sense of moral urgency. In part this was inevitable: the fever pitch of the 1930's, labor's heroic era, continued on to some extent through the period of our study, but this sense of high dedication could not continue indefinitely. Both McCarthyism, by inhibiting interest in social change, and television, by providing alternate forms of recreation, may have reduced the union's importance as a focal point in workers' lives.

Loss of Idealism

Union leaders seem to have lost much of the idealistic motivation which had made them so effective. Many men who were once inspired leaders have taken on the hardened cynicism of political ward bosses. Although most leaders are subtle bargaining technicians and skillful picket-line organizers, few demonstrate enough flexibility to adjust to changing conditions, particularly management's recent more sophisticated strategies.

Local leaders seem less willing to *give* time to their union. At the time of our study, it was not uncommon for local officers to spend as many as three nights a week at membership and executive committee meetings, all without compensation (see pp. 58–59). Today a growing number of unions *pay* their officers to attend meetings. Furthermore, there is considerable evidence of petty corruption, such as expense account padding, misuse of "lost time" allowances, and kickbacks on purchases of union supplies.

Difficulty in Recruiting new Blood

Most of the men who founded industrial unions in the "heroic" 1930's were in the twenty-five to forty-five age bracket. Today these men are at least in their fifties and sixties, and age is taking its toll. Generally, the average age of union leaders seems to be rising.

Unions are finding it difficult to recruit adequate replacements for the men who retire or die. The men described in Chapter 7 were dedicated, energetic, and highly competent. Had there been no depression, many would have been promoted into management or would have gone on to college. For them the union was an outlet for blocked aspirations—a chance both to express themselves and to serve an idealistic cause. Now there are fewer men of this sort among the ranks of hourly paid workers, and many of the best of these are offered management positions as soon as they show ability as union officers.

Many of those who do become active today look upon the union as an interesting hobby rather than a cause. Others run for office solely to bring themselves to management's attention as potential supervisors, to win super-seniority and protection against layoffs, or to represent the special interests of *their* work group as against others. The sense of common purpose described in Chapter 9 continues, but it is less strong.

Growing Management Sophistication

While union leadership seems to be getting weaker, management leadership is getting stronger. Industrial-relations departments have grown in size and are more fully accepted in the management structure. More important, a whole generation of college-trained men has taken over, displacing the old timers who had moved up through the ranks. Men are no longer selected for labor-relations work because they can get along with people or because they are useful elsewhere. Less emphasis is being placed on "making friends and influencing people," much more on ability to bargain and to engage in power politics. Some of these new men have master's degrees in industrial relations; almost all take a professional point of view toward their job.

At the time of our original study, we had the feeling in negotiations and arbitration proceedings that the union representatives were more skillful and better prepared than their management counterparts. Today, in sharp contrast with the case in the late 1940's, it is the management men who give the sense of knowing where they are going rather than of just drifting with the tide. Fifteen years ago, many industrial-relations directors looked upon themselves as mediators between union and management; privately they conceded their hardest job was to persuade foremen to get along with the union. Today, it is increasingly the industrial-relations department which is urging line management to be tough.

Automation and Unemployment

Automation and unemployment have been major threats throughout the period. Unions have been generally on the defensive, particularly during the depressed times of 1957–1962.

The spread of automation has made work rules into a major issue. As new processes are introduced, fewer men are needed; the individuals concerned try to protect their jobs, and the battle is joined. When these issues are dramatized as matters of principle, as they were during the 1959–1960 steel strike, high emotional feeling is inevitable. Slogans like "featherbedding," "speedup," "management prerogatives," "protection of job rights," and all the rest, are heard.

Yet automation is a creeping phenomenon and one about which it is difficult to formulate a clear union policy or to arouse clear membership support. Normally it effects only a few workers at a time (the railroad fireman's case is an exception). The strong and understandable desire of individual workers' to hold on to what they have encourages a certain amount of selfishness and makes unity behind job protection measures difficult to achieve. One steward explained:

> The members are divided on the basis of seniority. The high-seniority men are sitting pretty and don't pay much attention to the fact that men with lesser seniority are being laid off. They seem to say "it is not happening to me" and they close their eyes to what is happening.

Thus, automation greatly aggravates the internal differences described in Chapter 3.

Few unions are making an all-out effort today to stop technological change. Instead, industrial unions are seeking to cushion the impact of displacement through contractual demands for broader seniority, opportunities for retraining, severance pay, and "automation" funds (providing payments to men laid off because of technological change). Yet, not until recently were unions able to win membership support for even these proposals.

Management's Hard Line

In 1951, it looked as if industrial relations were entering into a period of working harmony in which management and union would collaborate increasingly in joint problem-solving. But by 1957 the picture began to change. Management reacted to union weakness and tight competitive conditions by trying to cut labor costs and by adopting a "hard line"—often called Boulwarism—in its dealings with unions. For a while, at least, top management showed a new sense of firmness and purpose in its dealings with unions. Its emphasis was no longer on "getting along" but on winning back some of the rights it had lost in the past. Employers increasingly tried to make bargaining a two-way street. Putting forth demands of their own, they sought to eliminate restrictive contractual provisions, and often engaged in strenuous public-relations campaigns to demonstrate the moral rightness of their cause to their employees and to the public generally.

Many labor-relations directors tried hard to restrict unofficial bargaining and to confine employee protests to the rigid structure of the grievance procedure. They sought to formalize procedures, to follow the contract to the letter, and to cut down sharply on the freedom of union stewards to circulate and collect grievances. High priority was given to the elimination of wildcat strikes and of the custom, which had developed in some companies, for men to refuse to carry out orders which they believed violated the contract. Efforts were made to train foremen in human relations and in the handling of grievances and also to eliminate the tendency to by-pass foremen in grievance handling.

Management's line seemed to be hardest about the time of the bitter 1959–1960 steel strike, which was fought over the issue of working rules. Since then, with renewed prosperity, labor relations seem to have mellowed. As of 1966, we see increasing evidence that many of the problems brought about by technological change are being resolved informally on a "problem-solving" basis without too much regard for past practices, explicit substantive contract terms, or contracturally prescribed methods of negotiation. But labor's power in the plant still seems somewhat weaker than it was in the early 1950's.

Intergroup Problems

Intergroup disputes have in many cases become more serious. Wage increases, given largely on a cents-per-hour basis, have tended to reduce the differentials enjoyed by skilled craftsmen, some of whom tried to form their own independent unions. The specter of unemployment made seniority issues more difficult to settle, while technological change, through eliminating some jobs and changing the nature of others, tended to upset job promotion ladders.

Rank-and-File Opinion

Someday we may have measures of fluctuations in member attitudes toward their union just as polling organizations now provide us with measures of fluctuation in voter attitudes toward presidential candidates as election time comes closer. The scattered evidence which we have at the moment suggests that most members still support their union, feeling that it is doing a good job for them and that they would be considerably worse off if it were to disappear.

To be sure, there are dissatisfactions in particular areas. In some cases union officers are looked upon as part of the "power structure," almost as unapproachable as management. In many plants there has been considerable frustration because unions have not succeeded in halting the march of automation. Yet, with a few significant exceptions, when the chips are down, in strikes or NLRB elections, the members do support their union, voluntarily and without coercion.

The exceptions are interesting. In 1960, General Electric workers returned to work after a few days on strike, ignoring their union's requests to stay off the job. Among professional-engineer groups, several have voted to decertify their union. And in contrast to the situation in the 1940's when workers gave 90 to 95 per cent to their unions in union shop elections, such elections held in West Coast areospace equipment plants in the early 1960's went relatively badly for unions, with voter support ranging from 54 to 74 per cent. Yet all these incidents involve special circumstances (which deserve closer study).

The Relative Position of the Local

For a while after 1951, it seemed as if the local was getting less important, as key collective bargaining decisions were increasingly being made at the level of the International union and the corporate industrial-relations department. Yet this trend was apparently carried too far, and many locals revolted after contracts were signed that ignored local problems. The issues most difficult to settle in recent steel and auto disputes have been at the local level, and the local union has been given greater autonomy in the settlement of these matters, even to the right to go on strike on their own.

*   *   *

Thus, the last fifteen years have brought substantial changes. Union leaders have lost some of their idealism and sense of dedication, and it has become harder to recruit effective replacements for those who retire or die. Management has become more sophisticated. Particularly during the period of the "hard line," it sought (not always with success) to restrict the types of un-official bargaining described in Chapter 2. Automation has created problems which unions find hard to solve. All these changes are important, and yet, in our opinion, they do not affect the essential validity of this book.

Recent Research

Not only have times changed since 1951, but also much important work has been published relating to union life.[2] This research centers on union member attitudes and participation and union democracy.[3]

Union Member Attitudes

Our analysis of the complex and ambivalent nature of union member attitudes still seems generally valid, although in recent years a great deal of

[2] For a comprehensive review of the literature until 1956 see Daisey L. Tagliacozzo, "Trade Union Government, Its Nature and Its Problems: A Bibliographical Review," *The American Journal of Sociology,* Vol. 61, No. 6 (May 1956), pp. 554–581.

[3] Mention should be made of Jack Barbash's survey of local unionism, *Labor's Grass Roots* (New York: Harper & Row, 1961). The footnote references in this book constitute a useful bibliography.

James W. Kuhn made an important contribution in his *Bargaining in Grievance Settlement: The Power of Industrial Work Groups* (New York: Columbia University Press, 1961). Kuhn makes use of the term "fractional bargaining" in elaborating upon the processes which we describe in Chapter 2.

work has been done using attitude surveys,[4] and contrasts have been made between member attitudes in different kinds of unions.[5] As might be expected, the attitudes of mineworkers and building trades workers—groups with long traditions of unionism—are very different from those of white-collar members. Efforts have also been made to identify various types of attitudes within a given union. One study distinguishes among "Patriots," "Gripers," "Pickers and Choosers," and "Fence Sitters"—each with a characteristic set of attitudes.[6]

Numerous authors have suggested that loyalty to one's union may not be inconsistant with loyalty to one's company.[7] In fact, "dual loyalty" to union and company may be merely an indicator of good social adjustment to one's work environment. In many cases, those who are most dissatisfied with their union are also dissatisfied with their company and are generally alienated from their job.

Finally, the available evidence supports our initial view that, though the average unionist' supports his union as an institution, he conceives of it as having rather limited objectives and, in psychological terms, as occupying a rather limited portion of his "life space."[8] He looks upon it as a service agency, but (with the possible exception of the case in craft unions) rarely identifies with it. To the disappointment of his officers, many of whom feel that political action is the best way of solving problems such as automation and look upon the union as a means of participating in the larger community, the average member feels his union should be strictly limited to the protection of economic interests. Certainly this average member does not see his union as a way of life.

All this helps explain why unions have been relatively unsuccessful in influencing their members' voting behavior.

Participation

Since 1951, there have been a great deal of systematic research dealing with various aspects of participation. It has become generally accepted that

---

[4] For example, Arnold S. Tannebaum and Robert L. Kahn, *Participation in Labor Unions* (Evanston, Ill.: Row, Peterson, 1958); and Arnold Rose, *Union Solidarity* (Minneapolis: University of Minnesota Press, 1952).

[5] For example, Joel Seidman, Jack London, Bernard Kersh, and Daisey Tagliacozzo, *The Worker Views His Union* (Chicago: The University of Chicago Press, 1958).

[6] Hjalmar and Rae Hudson Rosen, *The Union Member Speaks* (Englewood Cliffs, New Jersey: Prentice-Hall, Inc., 1955). See also Daisey L. Tagliacozzo, "A Typology of Rank-and-File Union Members," *The American Journal of Sociology,* Vol. 61, No. 6 (May 1956), pp. 546–553.

[7] Theodore V. Purcell, *Blue Collar Man* (Cambridge: Harvard University Press, 1960); "Dual Allegiance to Union and Management: A Symposium," *Personnel Psychology,* Vol. 7, No. 1 (Spring 1954), pp. 41–80.

[8] For example, Hjalmar Rosen and Rae Hudson Rosen, *op. cit.,* and an unpublished study, Institute of Industrial Relations, University of California, 1964.

a meaningful analysis of how unions work requires understanding of more than just formal participation, such as voting, attendance at meetings, officeholding, and going on strike. One must also consider forms of informal participation such as reading union newspapers, filing grievances, use of job pressures (such as slowdowns, speedups, obeying rules to the letter), as well as joining discussions of shop and union problems on the plant floor.[9]

On the basis of these more recent studies, we now have a considerably more sophisticated view of the participation process. Indeed, the analysis in our first edition has been considerably revised in this edition on the basis of further research by Sayles.[10] Probably the best single analysis of participation is that of Spinrad,[11] who examined numerous participation studies (including our original work) and, on the basis of these, concluded that, other things being equal, participation is likely to be higher among workers who:

1. Have jobs which provide significant opportunities for contact with other workers either at work or in union hiring halls

2. Live in isolated communities (such as miners or seamen) or at least live in neighborhoods where they are in close contact with their fellow workers

3. Have considerable leisure-time contacts with their fellow workers (perhaps because they work night shifts)

4. Are active in associations such as fraternal orders which are largely working-class in membership. (But participation will be lower if the associations to which they belong are primarily middle class.)

5. Belong to families or ethnic groups with union or socialist traditions

6. Are high in pay and status in a plant

7. Have satisfying jobs

8. Have a "positive orientation" toward their work situation and work group and view "their work group or the 'working class' or both as a significant reference group."[12]

To summarize further, Spinrad's analysis suggests that participation is a direct function of the level of (1) interaction with fellow workers on and off the job, (2) pay and status, and (3) satisfaction and identification with the job situation and one's fellow workers. However, as Sayles' recent work em-

[9] Joseph Kovner and Herbert J. Lahne conclude that we should think of participation primarily in terms of the informal shop society on the plant floor. (See their "Shop Society and the Union," *Industrial and Labor Relations Review,* Vol. 7, No. 1 (October 1953), pp. 3–14. While their point of view provides a useful corrective to the overemphasis on formal participation, to us it seems oversimplified.

[10] Leonard R. Sayles, *Behavior of Industrial Work Groups: Prediction and Control* (New York: John Wiley & Sons, 1958); Leonard R. Sayles, "Wildcat Strikes," *Harvard Business Review,* Vol. 32, No. 6 (October 1954), pp. 84–92.

[11] William Spinrad, "Correlates of Trade Union Participation," *American Sociological Review,* Vol. 25, No. 2 (April 1960), pp. 237–244. Spinrad relies to a considerable degree on Seymour Martin Lipset, Martin Trow, and James Coleman, *Union Democracy* (New York: Doubleday & Co., Anchor Books, 1962).

[12] *Ibid.,* p. 243.

phasizes, it also depends on (4) an ability to convert participation into meaningful gains. As Blau and Scott[13] put it:

> Putting these findings together, it becomes apparent that participation in labor unions is promoted not so much by resentment against management or more privileged groups as by positive identification with one's work, the work group, and the working class in general.

Democracy

We feel our analysis of union democracy is still very valid. Since 1952, there has been a great deal of discussion (scholarly and otherwise) about union democracy, in part inspired by the well-publicized McClellan hearings, which unearthed considerable evidence of corruption, racketeering, and undemocratic practices in many unions (but little in industrial unions—the type studied in this book).

For the most part, authors of recent studies have reached pessimistic conclusions.[14] They find unions relapsing into oligarchical control as they get older, and some scholars, echoing Dave Beck's contention that unions are essentially businesses selling labor, argue that unions have no need to be democratic.

Most of these studies deal primarily with the International level, and so it is tempting to dismiss them as irrelevant to our own study, since local unions seem to have relatively higher levels of officer turnover and sensitivity to membership pressures than do International unions. Yet, for reasons we have mentioned, even local unions seem to be suffering from spreading apathy and hardening arteries. The problem is serious, but in our opinion not as serious as some would make it.

Our main objection to many recent studies is that they utilize what we feel are unnecessarily and unrealistically stringent criteria for defining democracy. For example, in what is now one of the classic works of sociology, Lipset, Trow, and Coleman conclude that effective union democracy requires a two-party system.[15] In fact, at points they seem to assume that democracy and "the institutionalization of opposition" are synonymous.[16] Yet, the recent defeats of David McDonald as president of the Steelworkers Union and James Carey as president of the International Union of Electrical Workers provide dramatic evidence that long-entrenched leadership can be defeated, even in the absence of a well-defined, institutionalized two-party system. In

---

[13] Peter M. Blau and W. Richard Scott, *Formal Organizations* (San Francisco: Chandler, 1962), p. 48.

[14] See, for example, C. Peter Magrath, "Democracy in Overalls: The Futile Quest for Union Democracy," *Industrial and Labor Relations Review,* Vol. 12, No. 4 (July 1959), pp. 503–525.

[15] Lipset *et al., op. cit.*

[16] *Ibid.,* p. 13.

Britain the large Amalgamated Engineering Union is democratic in the sense that there are a large number of closely contested elections, yet there is no institutionalized two-party system in the sense that it exists in the ITU.[17]

Indeed, some have argued that a rough working democracy can be obtained in situations where the top leadership is re-elected year after year, provided the membership is able to influence policy. (After all, *what* the union does is more important than *who* does it.) Certainly some English unions give their top paid leadership life tenure, yet these unions are not noticeably less democratic than those with annual elections.

Few union leaders have their way all the time. Examine almost any union closely and you will discover numerous instances where the plans of top leadership have been modified in the face of lower level opposition—whether expressed openly on the convention floor, more discreetly in the smoke-filled atmosphere of closed executive council or convention committee meetings, or extraconstitutionally through wildcat strikes and the like. Even Jimmy Hoffa faced considerable opposition on the convention floor, and a great deal more was expressed very effectively in informal ways. What difference does it make if decisions on the convention floor are made with a ceremonial unanimity, provided these decisions reflect the balancing of various pressures behind the scene? (The interests of individuals not represented by pressure groups often get lost in the union, but it can be argued that this happens in the nation-state as well.)

Despite Michel's famous "iron law of oligopoly" there are also "compulsive pressures of democracy in unionism,"[18] strong beliefs by both the rank and file and the leadership that at least the trappings of democracy must be retained. Thus, bureaucratic decisions must be dressed in democratic garb and democratic, participative procedures used as a means of mobilizing support for leadership objectives. Indeed, Gouldner posits an "iron law of democracy" that no set of leaders can long flout the will of those it would control.[19]

And yet we are not fully satisfied with a "safety-valve" theory of union democracy—a theory which states that unions are democratic because, if things get *too* bad and the members become aroused enough, they have the power to change things. If unions are merely sellers of labor, this kind of democracy may be enough. But if unions are to serve as means by which workers participate in making vital decisions which affect them, then active participation, not just "safety-valve" democracy is required. Perhaps efforts should be directed toward preserving the more direct form of democracy at

[17] J. David Edelstein, "Democracy in a National Union: The British AEU," *Industrial Relations,* Vol. 4, No. 3 (May 1965), pp. 95–104.

[18] See the article having this as its title by John R. Coleman, *The American Journal of Sociology,* Vol. 61, No. 6 (May 1956), pp. 519–526.

[19] Alvin W. Gouldner, "Metaphysical Pathos and the Theory of Bureaucracy," *American Political Science Review,* Vol. 49 (1955), p. 506.

the local level, where the rank and file may participate. Bureaucracy at the International level may be less serious, provided this can be curbed by safety-valve techniques.[20]

In any case, taken as a whole there seems to be a good deal of democracy in the union movement. And in the mid-1960's, the degree of democracy (or political turmoil) seemed to be increasing rather than decreasing—helped in part by the Landrum-Griffin Act.

[20] Safety-valve democracy becomes more meaningful when there are safeguards to prevent the safety valve from sticking, such as the internal safeguards provided by impartial review boards established by the Auto Workers and the Upholsterers or the external safeguards provided by the Landrum-Griffin Act.

Index